ADITYANAMA

The Man behind the Banker Unveiled

Anita "Smiley" Puri

JAICO PUBLISHING HOUSE

Ahmedabad Bangalore Chennai
Delhi Hyderabad Kolkata Mumbai

Published by Jaico Publishing House
A-2 Jash Chambers, 7-A Sir Phirozshah Mehta Road
Fort, Mumbai - 400 001
jaicopub@jaicobooks.com
www.jaicobooks.com

ADITYANAMA
ISBN 978-93-93559-63-0

First Jaico Impression: 2023

Page design and layout by R. Ajith Kumar, Delhi

With Satguru's blessings

Sochai soch(i) na hovai
Je sochi lakh var
Chupai chup na hovai
Je lae raha liv tar
Bhukhia bhukh na utri
Je banna puria bhar
Sahas sianpa lakh hoi
Tu ik na chalai nal (i)
Kiv sachiara hoiai
Kiv kurai tutai pal (i)
Hukam (i) rajai chalna
Nanak likhia ral (i)

Human beings cannot comprehend God by thought alone, even by thinking (about Him) hundreds of thousands of times

One can keep silent and be absorbed in meditating on the divine and the love of God, but through silence alone, one cannot find inner peace

The lust, greed and hunger of the hungry is not appeased by piling up loads of worldly riches

Human beings may have plenty of clever schemes and cunning tricks but none of the cleverness will accompany them into the other world

How can I become true to myself? How must I smash the barrier of falsehood?

Follow the words of the divine, that is what Nanak says.

POT-PURI

WHEN I BEGAN WORKING ON THIS BOOK, I WAS ASKED repeatedly,"Why do you want to write this book?" Everyone I spoke to and discussed the idea with, has asked me this at some point in the conversation.

Frankly, I didn't have a ready answer at the time. This book is an emotional journey above everything else. And finding a rational answer for something like this is not easy, nor is it completely convincing. But the truth is that this book has been living inside me for so long that I needed to write it—there is no why or how I would do this, it simply had to be done.

Having said that, there are many reasons why I believe this book had to be written. For one, Aditya Puri, the banker, is well known and recognised the world over. We have all heard about his professional accomplishments and over the years, he too has expressed his views on business, banking and leadership through pieces in various publications.

However, this is not even a fraction of the man that Aditya truly is. I wanted to bring out the many facets to his personality through the several interesting and funny stories that I have about him and our life together. This would interest a lot of people and help them get to know Aditya's personality better. After all, a man is made up of so many parts. If we are to know a person, we must know what he is like at home, how he behaves with his family and with friends over and above his professional achievements.

For instance, Aditya always makes people laugh. He is always the first one in the family to see the funny side of things and constantly cracks jokes, which quite often, are at my expense! The result is that there is always laughter ringing through the house.

I don't feel that our marriage is more than four decades old at all. My life with Aditya has been like one big carnival. There has been non-stop entertainment on our journey, so much so that I haven't even had the time to stop and catch my breath at times. It has been like a whirlwind that has swept us all up in its arms—very joyous, full of action and many memorable moments that have gone by in a flash, even before I could say 'tickety-boo'.

Aditya has been there for me always. He is there to pick me up if I trip and he solves my problems promptly. So (by the grace of God), there have been no hiccups in our journey. His friends and colleagues have often remarked that it is because of Aditya that they have to face the ire of their wives at home; they demand to be pampered just the way that Aditya pampers me. He addresses me as 'Rani' or queen and frankly, I have always felt like the queen of his heart. He has spared me the stress and problems of his work life and has never let his professional commitments interfere with our time together—no matter what. We also share a lot of common interests and there are three that come to mind.

Trying new and different cuisines is very important to us and as you will see there are many interesting memories and stories that this has led to. We love going to different places and doing new things. We spend hours together just watching movies and shows on all the new OTT platforms.

Aditya's love for food is legendary. At home, we call him the executive chef—he wants to know what is on the menu, even tells you what should be on the menu, but never sets foot in the kitchen. He not only finds the best places to eat (which are usually tiny, roadside joints), but also makes sure that everyone tastes the food he loves.

He is a loving husband and father and an indulgent grandfather—our grandson Rian is the apple of his eye. For our son Amit and daughter Amrita, he has been a mentor and friend, someone they take their problems to, have a drink and share a joke with. Even now, they turn to him for advice about their careers.

There is never a dull moment when he is around. He is a prankster—always pulling my leg or pulling a fast one on friends and family. In our worst times and our best times, he makes sure that there is enough laughter and good food for company!

Being Mrs. Aditya Puri has been a great and joyful ride—a rich source and continuous supply of anecdotes and stories, which you will find in this book. They are funny, warm, emotional and extremely romantic moments and make for very interesting tales. I am sure they will bring a warm smile to your face and a chuckle to your lips and of course, help you know Aditya better. That was my intention in writing this book. He is an interesting person and being with him all these years has given me so much to share. But while I was sure that I wanted to write this book, it was not as easy convincing Aditya because he never liked drawing attention to himself.

Aditya has never liked the limelight so he resisted the idea of a book on him. Despite the intense media attention that came with the job and many international and national awards that he has won, he has remained a simple man. He lives a simple life, does not really enjoy large parties and his idea of a weekend well spent is relaxing at home with a drink and his family beside him.

Not once has he made us feel that he is special or that he should be treated differently. In fact, he has always said that his success is the result of teamwork, and that we must never boast about our achievements. The idea of a book was not something he was very keen on.

So the first time I wrote about him, I kept it a secret. I created a coffee-table book full of photographs, letters and memories from all over the world as a retirement gift for Aditya. I worked on the book during the months of the lockdown when Aditya was always at home and I had to be very careful of not letting him get even a whiff of what I was up to.

Given how alert and aware Aditya is as a person, it was not an easy task. But I managed to keep it under wraps despite all his questions. Phew, I have to say it was a relief when it was finished! When I gifted him the coffee-table book made specially for him, he was extremely emotional and he also saw how serious I was about doing this. That is how this project took wings and I was able to convince him to let me put the story of his amazing journey down on paper for others to read.

Arise, awake and do not stop until the goal is reached.
You have to grow from the inside out.
None can teach you, none can make you spiritual.
There is no other teacher but your own soul.
You cannot believe in God until you believe in yourself.

Swami Vivekananda

CONTENTS

Section 1: Love is in the air **1**

1. Marriages are made on the dance floor 3
2. Cupid strikes home 7
3. It happened one evening 11
4. Fate is a four-letter word 15
5. Dinner dates and driving lessons 22
6. Let's get married 26
7. Two Puris in a mandap 30

Section 2: Building a life together **35**

8. A home of our own 37
9. Love is a yo-yo on Juhu beach 42
10. Small talk 46
11. Life is an airport carousel 50
12. Al-Khobar via Athens 54
13. Coffee, wine and desert games 58
14. Flowers and feng-shui 63
15. A tree too far 69
16. Never a dull moment 74
17. A thankful heart 79

Section 3: Banker on the rise **83**
18. Home is where the heart is 85
19. Goodbye Kuala Lumpur, hello Mumbai 90
20. Doing it ourselves 95
21. A gift from the ocean 101
22. Starry skies and waterfalls 107
23. A ghost in the garden 112
24. A slice of history 116
25. Everybody knows Mr. Puri 122
26. Saying it like it is 127
27. The maharaja and I 130
28. Everyman's banker 134

Section 4: Home is where the heart lies **139**
29. The jewel in the desert 141
30. Karni Mata and her messenger rats 144
31. Wish lists 148
32. Tennis fans and swimming pools 152
33. Where there is a will… 156
34. Puzzles, football and cheat sheets 161
35. No frills, no fuss, no time for superstitions 165
36. An actress in our home 169
37. Two hearts beat in one-Part I 174
38. Two hearts beat in one-Part II 179

Section 5: The last word **183**
39. The complete man 185

40. The man we know 190
Mukesh Ambani 190
Anand Mahindra 191
Sunil Mittal 191
Mallika Srinivasan 192
Narayan Murthy 193
Uday Kotak 193
Nandan Nilekani 194
K V Kamath 195
N Chandrasekaran 196
Sanjiv Mehta 196

Family tree 199
Conclusion 201

Love is in the air

01

1

MARRIAGES ARE MADE ON THE DANCE FLOOR

THE SUN WAS DRAWING PATTERNS ON THE FLOOR, PLAYING hide and seek in the dark halls of Miranda House Hostel in New Delhi. The flowers were in full bloom, adding a burst of colour to the place and some warmth to the unusually wet and grey August afternoon. The year was 1972. I was a young 17-year-old fresher, watching the bustle of girls walking up and down. After nearly a month of running around between lectures to numerous administrative offices, I had managed to get into the highly coveted corridors of Miranda House Hostel and it was a relief to be sitting there that day, just watching the day roll by.

I looked up to see Deepa Capoor (now Khanna) striding purposefully towards me. Like me, Deepa was a fresher. But unlike me, a girl from Mumbai (then Bombay) who had done her schooling in the protective custody of Lovedale, Ooty, she was from Delhi and far more tuned in to the ways of this huge college and university. Although we had just met and barely knew each other, I liked her and found her confidence and familiarity with the place both refreshing and reassuring.

"Want to come to a party?" Deepa asked. Her cousin, who lived in Defence Colony, was organising one and had invited all of us, she said. Defence Colony, now a tony South Delhi enclave, was at the time a sleepy residential conclave of officers of the armed, naval and air forces. Eyes twinkling, Deepa promised that the party would be great fun, with good music, good food and lots of dancing and singing.

Here I was, barely getting to know my classmates in a new city and acutely missing home and parents. Plus, I had never really been to such a party. I was too stunned to react. All I could hear buzzing inside my head was: *What? A party. With boys. What would my dad say? Unthinkable.*

"Come on," Deepa said, "you will have a lot of fun." I didn't want to let her on to my fears. So, I said, "I don't think I can. There is a problem. How will I get a night out from the warden? You are not on my list of local guardians and they will throw me out of the hostel if they find out. No *baba*, I am not doing anything like this. As it is, I have got the hostel after so much trouble."

"Don't worry," she said, "I know how to manage these things." Little did I know that at the time Deepa would do anything to get me to agree—she had been given this mandate (a secret that I was let into many years later) by her cousin and my husband of over four decades, Aditya, to gather as many girls as she could for a party.

He had put together everything one needed for a good, boisterous party. The venue—his father's house in Defence-

Colony—was ready and his friends and the music had all been lined up. The only hitch was that he didn't know too many girls. "Invite your friends, the freshers from Miranda House," Aditya had instructed Deepa. With her cousin's urgent message in mind, she stood before me that August afternoon in 1972, hoping to convince me and others to join her.

I am often awestruck with the way fate worked its way in our lives and how this conversation and the evening out ended up changing the course of my life forever. But let me not get ahead of the story.

To go back to the evening in New Delhi, I was nervous, never really having gone to a 'dance party' before. But I was also looking forward to the novel experience. I was always up for meeting people and making new friends. I also wanted to get a feel of Delhi's night life, something I hadn't experienced till then.

As soon as we reached this really beautiful home, tucked away in a tiny lane with large houses and old trees, Deepa introduced me to Aditya. I don't remember much from that evening except that we never left each other's side. Neither he nor I had eyes for anyone else. Like it happens in the movies, everything around us faded into the background and we danced together the entire evening, spinning around the room with each other and no one else. Time stood still as we slid across the dance floor without a care for anything or anyone else in the room.

The party ended way too soon and Aditya and I parted without any idea of how we would meet or whether we'd meet ever again. When I bring this story up with my children or my young friends, they find it hard to believe. "What!? You didn't share numbers? You didn't arrange to meet again—how did you even think you could meet again?" To all of them I say, don't judge us by the times we live in now. This is well before the time of social media and mobile phones, frankly well before the time it was acceptable to go out on a date or choose your own life partner. For Aditya and me, however strong the attraction may have been that evening, we didn't know what to do with that feeling. Perhaps it was naivety or it was the manner of our upbringing, we did not plan to meet again.

I graduated three years later from Miranda House but I hadn't seen Aditya again after that evening at his father's house.

> "Love looks not with the eyes, but with the mind. And therefore, is winged Cupid painted blind."
>
> William Shakespeare
> *A Midsummer Night's Dream (Act 1, Scene 1)*

2

CUPID STRIKES HOME

"DO YOU KNOW A GIRL OF MARRIAGEABLE AGE, GOOD ENOUGH for my nephew?"

One rather humid afternoon in Ahmedabad, a group of women sat across a table dealing cards and swapping stories about their lives. My aunt (chachi or father's brother's wife), Sudarshan Chachi was there with some of her friends and her ears perked up at the question. She knew that my parents were looking for a suitable groom and given that the person asking her the question was one of her closest friends, she was naturally interested. "Who's the boy?" she asked.

More important for us and our story—who was her friend?

The year was 1977. The person asking the question was Usha Capoor. She is Aditya's aunt (bua or father's sister) and she knew our family well too. Usha Bua and Sudarshan Chachi were friends. There is another interesting family connection here that I find quite fascinating—Usha Bua's sister (also Aditya's aunt) was married to Manohar Kampani (in the relationship matrix, he is Aditya's phoophaji or uncle) who had been instrumental in helping my grandparents safely across the border into India during the horrific days of the partition of the country.

Both our families were originally from undivided Punjab and had to flee their homes, leaving everything behind during the Partition of 1947. Originally from Sargodha (now in Pakistan), Aditya's great grandfather, Rai Bahadur Lala Brij Lal Puri, had shifted to Chandigarh when the countries were divided into two. My grandparents had also made the move to India around the same time and later, my parents found their way to Mumbai and settled down in the western part of the country. Lala Brij Lal Puri stayed in the northern part of the country. The ties between the two families ran deep. More importantly, for our story, Aditya's aunt, Usha Bua, and my aunt, Sudarshan Chachi, were close friends and they happened to be at the right place at the right time.

Neither aunt knew about our meeting in Delhi, nor did they know that Aditya had spent the better part of the last few years trying to track me down. He had reached out to his cousin Deepa several times asking about me and she had finally thrown up her hands in despair saying that we were not in touch anymore.

Deepa even ticked him off for being so foolish. She had snapped back at him saying, "Why didn't you speak up when you had the opportunity? Now after all these years, where am I going to find her for you?"

Deepa was living in Mumbai and was now married to Uday Khanna. I was in Mumbai too, living with my parents, but neither knew that we lived in the same city. And while she set up a search for me, my parents had accelerated their search for a suitable groom.

After coming back from Delhi, I had signed up for a travel and tourism course at Nirmala Niketan. Tourism was still new and untested as a potential business opportunity. Courses such as the one that I had enrolled for were just about beginning to find a wider audience. It helped me land a job with Japan Airlines(JAL), but unfortunately my stint there was short-lived. JAL shut down three months after I joined and I looked out for a new opportunity while my parents began hunting for a groom for me.

My father was not keen that I work, but I was adamant and we finally struck a deal—if I did manage to get a job on my own, he would not stand in the way but he was not going to help me find one. My parents were quite sure that a groom would be easier to get than a job!

Jobs were hard to come by at the time and there were usually hundreds of applicants for every position. As luck would have it, Kuwait Airlines advertised for a position and I sent in my application. I knew that there wasn't an easy way in. I had to find a way to make my candidature special.

It seemed like a good idea to learn Arabic. After all, how many applicants in Mumbai would know the language? *Surely this would give me an edge*, I thought. There was a short window of three months before the interview and I put it to good use. It worked and I began life as a working woman in the metropolis. The daily commute to Nariman Point from my home in Pali Hill offered me independence that I quite enjoyed.

For my parents however, the pressure to find a husband for their youngest daughter kept mounting, just as it did for Aditya's parents. Aditya had been turning down numerous proposals, putting his mother in extremely awkward situations and his cousin Deepa in a spot over his insistence that she find me.

Aditya's mother finally served him an ultimatum, asking him to find a bride for himself if he didn't like who his parents had chosen for him.

Imagine the surprise when one day Deepa received a call from her mother (Usha bua) asking her to find out about this girl called Smiley who lived in Mumbai! Deepa nearly dropped the phone receiver. Even though she was still unsure if this was the same girl she had been looking for at her brother's behest, she felt that she had found the 'one' (After all how many Smileys could there be in this world and wanting to get married?!). Within minutes, she was on the line with Aditya, yelling excitedly into the receiver: "I think I found your Smiley!"

> "Lovers don't finally meet somewhere.
> They're in each other all along."
>
> Jalal-Al-din-Rumi

3

IT HAPPENED ONE EVENING

THE RAINS HAD LASHED THE CITY INTO A STATE OF COMPLETE submission. The roads had disappeared under large pools of water and it took me nearly three hours to get home that evening. All my plans of dressing up for the big evening, the day that Aditya and I were to officially meet for the first time, were completely wiped out.

I barely managed to step out of my wet office-wear into something more appropriate and was ruing the fact that I had not left earlier or even better, taken the day off. Frankly, I need not have bothered because the man who had spent the better part of the past few years looking for me refused to speak to me that evening. Not a word!

I was furious. I told my sister that I am never getting married to this man; he was so arrogant that he didn't utter a word. Who does he think he is?

Unfortunately, my fury went unnoticed by everyone in the family. Aditya was quite the 'catch' as we would say at the time. He belonged to a respected Punjabi family with deep ties to our family, as I pointed out earlier. The Puris were highly regarded in Chandigarh where his grandfather had settled and his father Tapishwar Puri had served as the aide de camp to the first Indian Chief of the Air Staff, Subroto Mukherjee. Aditya himself had several factors going in his favour; he had made it to the merit list in the Indian chartered accountancy exams and was working with a global bank.

In my father's eyes, there could hardly ever have been a better match for me. Being a businessman himself, he didn't want his daughters to be subjected to the vagaries of households which relied on business for income. He had repeatedly stated his desire for a son-in-law who held a steady job and brought home a regular pay every month. A banker was at the top of his list of suitable boys and that too one who worked for a multinational bank.

My irritation dissipated sooner than I could even acknowledge it fully. This was my first brush with the Aditya Puri way of doing things—once he knows his mind, he spends no time dithering over a decision. I was unaware that Aditya was so sure that he wanted to marry me that he didn't think it necessary to ask any questions.

He knew he wanted the girl he had lost his heart to, all those years ago that evening at his parents' home, to be his wife. All he was really doing that dark rainy evening in July 1977 was confirming that I was the Smiley he had been looking for. Once he was sure of that, he wasted no time sweeping me off my feet into a whirlwind courtship, quick engagement and a wedding that followed *tout de suite.*

He had shown similar nerve and boldness in carving a place for himself in the big, busy city when he first moved here from Delhi.

Aditya had come to Mumbai in 1974, with a job in Mahindra and Mahindra as an executive assistant to its finance director. He lived as a paying guest in Colaba in South Mumbai and his office was in Kandivali, a distant western suburb. After a few months of braving the maddening crowds every morning on the local trains, he found himself looking for better opportunities. He was also growing tired of his paying guest accommodation because the street on which he lived was not the best street to be on. It was dimly lit and, in the evenings, it was impossible to walk down without being accosted by soliciting women of all ages.

Aditya was used to a very different lifestyle in Chandigarh. They had a palatial home and all the comforts of life were laid out for him. He was spoilt thoroughly by his paternal grandparents who doted on him. But now, in the tiny room where he lived, the landlady gave him half a bucket of water to bathe in every morning and half a cup of tea and a biscuit for breakfast. The food was nothing to write home about and the place itself was a dump.

One can imagine what a sharp contrast it was to the life Aditya had left behind. In a new city, everything was a struggle. One evening when he sat watching the lights on the city's iconic Marine Drive, he said, "Bombay, we are not friends now, but will be friends one day."

Soon thereafter, Aditya found a job at Citibank and that changed his life. No more living in rooms that barely had room to stand up in. No more elbowing one's way into crowded trains that sapped all the life out of daily commuters. He now lived in one of the priciest neighbourhoods in town, off Warden Road, on Bomanji Petit Road in South Mumbai and had much more time for himself as the commute to and from work had reduced considerably.

How did Aditya break into the elite club of multinational bank employees? How did he, a newly-minted chartered accountant who was also new to the city, find a foothold in the cutthroat and competitive world of banking? Now, that makes for a whole new story.

“A good head and a good heart are always a formidable combination.”

Nelson Mandela

4

FATE IS A FOUR-LETTER WORD

AMONG YOUNG BACHELORS OF A CERTAIN VINTAGE IN MUMBAI, the late Dorothy Ganapati held legendary status. Her name may not be familiar outside the elite circles of the city, but in Mumbai of the early 1970s, she truly was a force to reckon with.

Ms. Ganapati lived in a fancy, art deco building opposite the iconic Oval Maidan. She lived in a large, spacious and airy apartment where she took in paying guests at a fraction of the rent that other places sought but offered more than anyone else in the market. On offer was a lavish breakfast, an occasional cognac after dinner on weekends and meals that spread over many courses and were served on expensive cutlery. What more could the young and newly employed in the city want? But her largesse came with a condition. All paying guests had to play Scrabble with her at 8 p.m. every Saturday!

Strange as it may seem to many, it posed no problems at all for Aditya who had grown completely tired of his old, dingy paying guest arrangement. When he and his roommate heard about Dorothy Ganapati and her apartment, they jumped at the offer. A game of Scrabble was hardly any sacrifice at all if it meant trading up to a better room, better location and better food.

It turned out to be a great experience. The rooms were clean and well-kept and the food, something that has always been and continues to be a big weakness for Aditya, was outstanding. On weekends, breakfast was a grand spread. They had fresh juice, bacon, fried egg, rare coffee brews and in the evening, a bottle of cognac would be brought to the table after their meals.

Aditya still recounts stories of how he was ignorant when it came to fine dining. He learnt the nuances of taste, flavour and presentation under the sharp-eyed tutelage of Ms. Ganapati. How else would anyone know that chili sherry was something that stirred in some tanginess into your soup and not a liquor to be swirled in a glass. Every day came with a new discovery and a taste of a new and exciting life—but there was a rider.

Every Saturday, come hell or high water, there would be a game of Scrabble waiting for them. It was lovely company and an enjoyable game too, but the routine soon grew tedious. And the weekends were a complete washout. Here were two young men, kick-starting their working life in a city famous for its night life, but they were unable to experience any of it. Things had to change and call it what you will, destiny or just chance, they soon did.

One day, Aditya got a call from his cousin, Bikram Kochchar, who had just joined Citibank India. Bikram was in town and wanted to catch up over a drink. Given Aditya's work hours at Mahindra & Mahindra and his living arrangement, it was decided that they would meet at a restaurant. It was through him that Aditya got to know about Citibank and the lifestyle it offered its young recruits. As Aditya made his way back home that evening, he had just one desire playing on loop—a job with Citibank. It overrode every other dream he may have had about his future until then.

As a first step, Aditya knew he had to find his way into an interview room with the big bosses at Citibank. Luckily for him, there was a team from the bank working with Mahindra & Mahindra on a joint project at the time. And soon a meeting was set up with the renowned Nanoo Pamnani, who was the country head of Citibank at the time.

I have to say here that Nanoo has played a big part in our lives. First as Aditya's boss and mentor, and then as a friend and guardian to both of us. Anyway, going back to the interview room that day, Nanoo grilled Aditya very closely. He had come highly recommended from colleagues who had worked on the joint project. Still, Nanoo wanted to see for himself if all that he had heard about Aditya was really true.

There was someone else batting in Aditya's favour with Nanoo—his wife, Chitra. She also worked with Citibank and had watched Aditya very closely whenever he would go to the bank as a client (Mahindra & Mahindra). She dispelled any doubt Nanoo may have had about Aditya's capabilities because she told him that he was able to understand both sides of the problem better than most.

Satisfied that he had found the right person for the job, Nanoo made Aditya an offer. And within weeks, Aditya had swung his way into the job of his dreams. Not just that, he had also managed to double his salary. When Nanoo made the offer at first, he had pencilled in a 50 per cent increase in money. But Aditya, never averse to taking a calculated risk, said, "I am already getting this.

Why should I make the jump for the same terms?" And Nanoo agreed and gave him the appointment letter and set him on the path for a training programme in Beirut.

The stint at Beirut was something that changed Aditya's life completely. The first evening, he along with other newly recruited Citibankers bought a bottle of Black Label whisky, which used to be every young man's dream alcohol at the time. He bought an Omega watch too, for himself—his first branded purchase. It was like a small town boy eagerly experiencing all that big city life had to offer.

Soon after returning from Beirut, Aditya would find himself accommodation in the Citibank chummery in one of the priciest parts of South Mumbai. Life was looking up for the young man who had despaired of finding a decent home in the city and whose search for his 'Smiley' had yielded nothing but disappointment so far.

It is at this point that we reentered each other's lives—he worked with Citibank and I worked with Kuwait Airways. It turned out to be a boon for us because the Kuwait Airways office was in Nariman Point—just a hop, skip and a jump away from the Citibank office. One afternoon, actually just the day after our 'arranged' meeting at my sister's house where he had refused to acknowledge my presence, Aditya landed up at my workplace.

I was working when I heard my name called out over the speaker. A visitor for you, I was informed. Outside, a sea of faces stared back at me. "Anyone for me?" I asked, identifying myself to the crowd when Aditya stepped in front of me. I almost fell over in shock. One, I was livid with his behaviour the previous evening and secondly, we didn't go about meeting each other like that those days. This was well before dating became acceptable and especially among families like mine (a Punjabi business family steeped in tradition), such meetings were unheard of.

"What are you doing here?" I asked.

"I want to take you out," he said.

He must be crazy. "Have you asked my father? How can I come with you without his permission? Do you know he will never let me out alone with you?!" I let off a volley of questions. Aditya was unfazed. Now we often have a laugh about how many times I invoked the name of my father in that conversation but at the time, he simply heard me out.

If a permission was what I needed, he was going to get that and Aditya reached out to Avinash, my sister Ritu's husband. Avi intervened on our behalf and also agreed to be our chaperone and only then did my father let me go with Aditya for our first date (not counting the evening on the dance floor!).

We went to The Oberoi, a swanky five-star property just off Marine Drive in South Mumbai. Avi gallantly agreed to leave us alone as we hopped off to the bar and restaurant on the rooftop.

"Are you being forced into marriage?" That was Aditya's first question as we settled down with our drinks. It caught me unawares and I said, "Arre, no! Why should I be afraid of marriage? Everyone gets married and I also want to settle down. My father says I have to settle down, so I have to settle down."

Rolling his eyes at my continuous reference to my father, he prodded further. "Are you scared of marriage?" I laughed. Marriage is like breathing or eating. My rather large extended family of uncles and aunts were walking-talking advertisements for marital bliss and had instilled in me a desire for marriage and family life.

"Scared! Why should I be scared? One is afraid of a rat or something, but not marriage," I scoffed. My answer must have amused him and also reassured him because he did not pursue it further and we spent an enjoyable evening chatting and discovering many interesting things about each other.

Decades later, Aditya in the true nature of the prankster-storyteller that he is, has turned this episode on its head. He always winks at his friends and drops his voice to a low whisper before quipping, "She was always the wise one. She knew that she had nothing to be afraid of but the one who should have been scared that evening was me!"

Avi tells an interesting anecdote about these days. He was sent to meet Aditya at the Citibank chummery before he came over to our house for the official meeting. Aditya told him, "I am interested in marriage, but I can't afford a wife yet." To that Avi replied, "Well, my father still says he cannot afford a wife!"

We met a few more times before we were engaged at the roka ceremony (this means that the couple is committed to each other) as is the tradition in Punjab. Aditya's parents who had a liberal and non-traditional approach to life didn't see me until the roka ceremony—if their son was happy, they were happy to go along with him. In fact, Aditya's father, Tapishwar Puri, shocked my father when he said that there was no need for any roka ceremony—just let the boy and girl exchange a laddoo each and be done with it.

My father was having none of that. He wanted the world to know that his daughter had been betrothed to this young, handsome boy who worked in a multinational bank. We had a big ceremony to announce our engagement to the world. Little did my father know that this was probably the last time he would get the upper hand when it came to dealing with his son-in-law and his unconventional ways!

> “I am the master of my fate,
> I am the captain of my soul.”
>
> William Ernest Henley
> *Invictus*

5

DINNER DATES AND DRIVING LESSONS

NEW TO THE CITY AND FRESHLY INDUCTED INTO CITIBANK with a fiancée in tow, Aditya thought that this was a good time to take up driving lessons. He was a novice behind the wheel while I drove my father's car quite regularly to the Citibank chummery at Lynwood House near Parsi General Hospital, where he lived at the time. We decided that I would be his driving instructor and use my dad's car for his lessons. It was a good opportunity for us to spend more time together and get to know each other better.

But before I tell you about our driving lessons, I have to spend some time telling you about the time we spent at Lynwood House. Those are unforgettable days and have left behind so many memories.

The apartment was huge, spacious and everyone had a room of their own. The residents, as employees of a premier multinational bank, enjoyed perks that few could even dream of at the time. The furnishings, the rooms, the crockery and the lifestyle, everything was a big upgrade for Aditya.

Aditya's life in the chummery was as good as it could get for young trainee executives in the big city. His place, as I have probably said before, was located in the best part of town. Citibank had also employed a butler to look after the residents. His name was Paul and he was very fond of all the residents and always had a gleam in his eye, like he knew just what the residents of the house were really up to all the time.

I still believe that Paul thoroughly spoilt all the young men staying at the chummery. He made sure that the boys walked into a room that had been cooled down sufficiently every evening, he would keep the air conditioner on for an hour or so before they came back. He did the laundry and put it away neatly folded in their cupboards. And, the most impressive thing of all, he made sure that the bathwater was the perfect temperature, before any of them stepped into the bathtub!

Paul was a brilliant cook and once to impress me, Aditya asked him to dish out a huge continental meal. The table groaned under the weight of the food that Paul had prepared; pot roasts, bakes and desserts and everything laid out in the best cutlery. He had even given him instructions that Paul should make himself present as soon as he was called just because '*Memsaab ko* impress *karna hai*' (I have to impress the lady).

Aditya's efforts backfired badly. I was so intimidated by Paul's efficiency—the way he laid out the table and the food he cooked, that for the first time, I began wondering if I had bitten off more than I could chew. Marriage was not as much of a scary proposition for me as the thought of having to cook and clean and keep house like Paul.

I had grown up in a simple Punjabi business family. We never bothered with such matters. But I have come to learn that Aditya treasures these practices. And frankly, now so do I. Back then, when I saw the style and panache with which the chummery was looked after, for the first time since I had met Aditya, the prospect of a married life set butterflies in my stomach.

However, Aditya was able to put me at ease very quickly—his charm worked on me always as it does even now!

Getting back to the story of being his driving instructor, Aditya was a quick learner and an eager one. We were soon making quite good progress too, cruising the streets around Lynwood House over the weekends and also on the odd holiday that we managed to spend together. It was quite a smooth ride until we decided to get a bit adventurous and take the car out of the confines of the driving boundary that we had set for ourselves.

One day we skipped the regular route and spun our way into the adjoining roads. These were busy roads and had several large colleges and hospitals around them. Aditya had just about mastered the art of braking and accelerating smoothly, but still had to learn how to manoeuvre the car up and down slopes.

Ask anyone familiar with the city, especially one who has driven around this part of town and they will tell you that we were setting ourselves up for trouble. Not only were we headed into a busy road, it was also one that looped up and down around the area, with several intersections and signals thrown in. In short, if we didn't know how to ride up and down a slope, we should not have been there.

As we drove out of Warden Road and headed towards Hughes Road, Aditya brushed up against a car, grazing it mildly. Its driver went red in the face and began abusing us loudly. Flustered and confused, Aditya stepped on the accelerator and instead of moving away, we just went closer to the car that we had scratched and worsened the damage.

The man was livid and began yelling at us. Though we were sorry and kept apologising profusely, his parting repartee had us doubling over in laughter. "Must be your father-in-law's car, it is not your money that is going down the gutter but his," he screamed and followed it up with the choicest of cuss words. If only he knew he had hit the nail on the head.

> "By three methods we may learn wisdom:
> First, by reflection, which is noblest;
> Second, by imitation, which is easiest; and
> third by experience, which is the bitterest."
>
> Confucius

6

LET'S GET MARRIED

"YOU KNOW HOW MUCH MONEY I HAVE IN MY ACCOUNT? FIVE thousand rupees. Know that I can take good care of you." Aditya had picked me up from work and we were headed towards Marine Drive when he said this.

Ask him today and he grins sheepishly at his confidence. He was living in the big city, had a good job and life was looking up for him with Citibank where he was not only working hard but earning well and also travelling abroad, a rarity in India at the time. Little did he know that I was used to a far more luxurious lifestyle. But money does not matter at all in the heady days of courtship when we were busy getting to know each other and I was not really bothered about how much he had in his bank account.

Aditya said that we should just get to know each other for a few years before getting married. He had told Avi that he was in no rush; the job at Citibank had opened up a whole new world for him and he wanted to savour every moment.

I didn't really see any problem with that, but my father was not pleased. He had to get his daughter married. He had finally found the right boy and waiting made no sense to him. Luckily for him, Aditya soon gave up on the waiting game.

Those days he would drop me back home every evening. I lived on Pali Hill, a neat and cozy part of Bandra, a western suburb in Mumbai and he lived off Warden Road. He wanted to impress me, having already told me about his hefty bank balance and we would take a cab every day. But a taxi ride burnt a neat hole in his pocket and as the bills began mounting up, marriage seemed a much more attractive proposition than a long courtship. "Let's get married," he told me one day. "I can't afford these long taxi rides and I can't not be with you either."

My father was only too happy about Aditya's change of heart while his friends teased him that they knew his goose had been cooked long before he would admit it to himself. He was fooling no one but himself with all his talk of 'getting to know each other better'.

They had been telling him so ever since the famous New Year party, 31 December 1977. New Year's eve was something of a tradition at the Citibank chummery. Spacious, always well-stocked with alcohol and food and with adequate help around, it had become an annual ritual to host a grand all-nighter at the house. That year, I was a new attendee and while we were dancing and singing our hearts out, I was also aware that I had to go home to my parents. It was a tradition at my house for the family to get together to bring in the new year.

When I told Aditya this, I could have cut the silence in the room with a knife. His friends were sure that this was a deal breaker—a man who partied even harder than he worked was not going to turn into a Cinderella for his own party, or would he? I had no idea about all this and I kept telling him that we need to go back before the clock struck twelve as my parents would be waiting for us. Finally, he left with me. The next day, his flatmates lost no opportunity to tell him that he had signed the death warrant on his bachelorhood and that Smiley had hooked and anchored him for life.

With Aditya coming around to an early wedding, my father was only too happy to set the date and he got ready for the grand wedding of his youngest daughter. His last responsibility had to be performed with all the pomp and grandeur that one associates with big fat Punjabi weddings. Both he and my mother had been preparing for the task at hand for months. But as I have said earlier, Aditya's unconventional ways had begun to upturn everything in my life and the wedding was no exception.

Aditya said that the wedding would have to be a simple ceremony and just a handful of people would be invited. Not more than 8–10 people from his family would come, he declared as he did not believe in grand gestures that wasted money. Like I said, life with Aditya has been anything but conventional!

My father was stunned, not only because that is not how Punjabi families conducted their affairs but also because my sister's wedding had been a huge affair. Her wedding six years ago had the groom riding an elephant and a mandap that lit up half of Jaipur! But Aditya was adamant and even if I had wished for a fancy wedding with multiple parties and many people, I kept my desires to myself.

We got married at the Arya Samaj Mandir in Santacruz and just 8–10 people came from his family. It was a simple wedding with no frills and it was followed by a honeymoon in Goa. My parents came around to his view and his parents gave in too. They were all happy that Aditya had finally agreed to a marriage and that he had found the girl of his dreams. But our wedding ceremony, small and intimate though it was, was not without its own set of twists and turns.

> "A journey of a thousand miles begins with one step."
>
> Old Chinese proverb

7

TWO PURIS IN A MANDAP

IT WAS MY FATHER'S LONGSTANDING DESIRE THAT HE HAVE a banker as a son-in-law. He had told me often that running one's own business brought with it its own set of problems and financial insecurities, so he wanted his daughters to have none of that. A banker was respected, brought home a steady income and kept regular work hours—all necessary ingredients for a happy life, in my father's book.

Aditya more than met his expectations of a dream son-in-law on that front, but when it came to my father's idea of a wedding and its associated ceremonies and traditions, Aditya broke every rule in his book. From wanting to take his daughter out unchaperoned on dates before the *roka* ceremony to having a small wedding, he challenged every expectation that my father had set for the wedding ceremony of his youngest child.

If my father had his way, he would have pulled out all the stops for a wedding that screamed opulence and grandeur. If not elephants at the mandap, as he had done for my sister, he would have liked a five-star ceremony and invited the entire city.

Aditya had a simple question: "Why do you want to spend your father's hard-earned money on a wedding?" He would much rather that the money be saved and used for something more fruitful. My father could do little but go along with the rather practical wishes of his (still to-be) son-in-law because my family had begun to understand that once Aditya made up his mind there was little to stop him and no amount of cajoling would make him budge. I gave in too, but many years later, I made him more than make up for not going through the fun of a big fat Punjabi wedding. But that is a story I will tell you later—of how thirty years into our marriage we got married with pomp, ritual and splendour.

We were also getting used to another side of this headstrong young man, it was that of an irreverent and playful prankster—always ready to draw a few laughs out of every situation. But none of us had an idea of just how serious Aditya was about his pranks until our wedding day. We laugh about it today, but at the time all I remember was that my face was stinging with embarrassment and my family was aghast at the nonconformist *jamai* (son-in-law) who was coming into their family.

We were married on 28 January, 1978 at Arya Samaj Mandir, a nondescript temple cum community hall in Santacruz, off Linking Road, one of the busiest streets of the western suburbs at the time. It was just a short distance from my home and as planned, a small group of *baraatis* (guests that accompany the groom) had made their way to the venue. My family was present too, with just a few friends; my father had managed to sneak in a few, despite Aditya's stern warnings. After some last-minute glitches that threw us into a tizzy, it was time for the exchange of garlands or what is known as the *jaymala* in Punjabi weddings.

We stood facing each other—me in my red pure Tanchoi sari that had been chosen carefully by my sister and mother from Kala Niketan at Marine Lines, the biggest store in Mumbai for sarees at the time and him in his smart suit. Just as I got ready to garland him, Aditya stepped away. "No way is this going to happen without a kiss," he declared. I blushed red, pink and purple and I don't know how many colours, all at the same time. But Aditya was adamant. There were giggles, raised eyebrows and some lowered eyes (among the older family members) but Aditya stood his ground. No kiss, no *jaymala*.

I quickly stood on tiptoe and pecked him on his cheek but the mischief maker that he was, he said that won't do. I want a better one, he declared, his eyes twinkling as he knew just how awkward it was for me. Well, what does one do, you tell me? I shut my eyes and kissed him on his cheek without waiting for anyone to say anything, and quickly exchanged garlands to finally be pronounced a married couple.

Our wedding was an eventful affair, even if it was a small one. As we waited in the mandap for the pandit (the priest who would conduct the ceremony) to start the process, I saw my parents getting upset. Hurried discussions between the various elders followed and everyone was talking at the same time. They were all talking to the pandit, who kept shaking his head, saying, "A Puri cannot marry another Puri."

It turned out that the priest was taken unawares by the fact that we shared a surname and he refused to preside over a ceremony as he considered that to be against his principles! No amount of convincing worked. The diminutive old man was adamant. We thought that we may have to call off the wedding, until a rather smart solution presented itself. Now I don't remember if the priest offered the way out or it was some wise aunt, but it was decided that for the purposes of the wedding and the *kanyadaan* (a ceremony where one hands one's daughter over to the groom), I would be given away by my sister, Ritu. She had married into a family with the last name Dutta and hence did not break the pandit's ground rule about not betrothing two people with the same surname. Six years my senior, my sister had been more like a mother to me and I had followed in her footsteps all my life. It was a win-win all around.

My didi (sister), took me aside after the wedding and said, "I am thrilled that you have found a man like Aditya, but let me warn you it is not going to be easy. You will need to tame the 'shrewa' she said, given his fondness for pulling a fast one on everyone. He will be a handful, she said, but he will also make you happy."

Finally, the rather eventful wedding ceremony came to an end and Aditya and I were swiftly whisked off to the Taj Hotel. Antonia Shusta, who was heading Citibank's consumer banking division globally at the time had booked us for the night into the most expensive room in the hotel, as a wedding gift. I was over the moon, and over the years, we have lived in far bigger and more expensive hotels all over the world, but frankly the charm of that night that Citibank had arranged for us will remain forever etched in my mind.

"Raise your words, not voice
It is rain that grows flowers, not thunder."

Jalal-Ad-din Rumi

Building a life together

02

8

A HOME OF OUR OWN

OUR FIRST HOME WAS IN KHURSHEEDABAD, A QUAINT Citibank-owned building in the upscale neighbourhood of Altamount Road in Mumbai. It was a company apartment and quite a large one at that. Both of us struggled to furnish the house, burning large holes in our rather meagre pay packets as we bought beds and curtains and some other basic furniture.

We had moved in soon after our honeymoon, a few days spent on the rain-drenched beaches of Goa. I was happy to be living in the same city as my parents and sister. I routinely sought my sister's help in selecting the right shade of colour for the curtains, or finding the perfect place for budget furniture.

This was our first home together and even though we have moved 19 homes since, the joy of doing it up and its memories never fade. Everything we did held special meaning. For instance, I remember looking at the huge windows of the house and wondering how I would ever find enough fabric for curtains! I remember learning how to cook, how to keep a neat home and live on a budget, and everything we did, or planned, we did it together.

Another unforgettable memory from our early days is Kalam Singh–a cook, butler and man-of-all trades. He had come to live with us at my mother-in-law's insistence. To this day, Aditya jokes that he was the dowry his parents had to pay to bring me home as a bride. Kalam Singh cooked and kept house for us and was an absolutely delightful person to have around the house.

Those were heady days. Aditya was making a name for himself as a banker with Citibank. He worked hard and was getting recognised by his seniors in India and abroad. Despite his gruelling schedule, Aditya never let work come in the way of our personal life. Come what may, he was out of the office by 5:30 p.m. He never missed our evening ritual of tea, followed by a walk around the neighbourhood.

This is something that he continued to do throughout his life. Two principles that he held close from the start and that helped him, I think, become the person that he did were his punctuality—he is never late for a meeting even though he never wears a watch or carries a mobile phone and, his ability to make time for his personal and family life.

In all his years of work, be it at Citibank or HDFC Bank, Aditya tries his best to keep his evening for his family. However, he never leaves work on the table and if there is a deadline to be met or a crisis at work, he is one of the team. There are days when he comes home and continues to work until he has resolved the issue. And frankly, he never stops thinking about the bank—he would always look for a new idea or a unique business proposition. It is as if you can take Aditya out of the bank but the bank does not ever leave Aditya.

However, I have to add that his ability to leave at 5:30 p.m. every day has also led to some hilarious situations.

There is this story that he often recounts. It is from his days in Kolkata where Citibank had stationed Aditya for a few months. One day his boss called him aside and asked him in a serious undertone if there was something he wanted to talk about. "Is there a problem," he asked, "at home or at office?" Aditya was perplexed. "Nothing worrying me, sir, I am doing my work and leaving office on time. In fact, it gets dark by the time I manage to get out," Aditya told him.

His boss watched him with a smile curling around the corners of his mouth. "This is Calcutta (as the city was then called)," he quietly told him. "It gets dark by 4 p.m. in the winters." After that Aditya no longer relied on the light outside his window but checked the office clock before he packed off for the day.

Ask him how he manages to leave office early every day and his reply is that people should just stop confusing working hard with working late. People stay back to please the bosses or, because they feel obliged to hang out with their colleagues. All this is a waste of time and an inefficient use of the organisation's resources, is Aditya's stock answer.

While his attitude has won him high praise, it has also got him into trouble. Or perhaps I should say, got his friends and bosses into trouble. As it so happened with the late Nanoo Pamnani, mentor and friend and also the man who hired Aditya at Citibank.

When we were living in Khursheedabad, Nanoo lived on the first floor of the same building. I was pregnant with Amit and every evening, as was our habit, Aditya and I would step out for an evening walk. By the time we came back, we would see Chitra, Nanoo's wife at the balcony and stop for a chat. "So, Nanoo not back yet?" Aditya would ask Chitra, fully aware that Nanoo was still at work. When she nodded a no for an answer, he would remark, "You will have to talk to Nanoo why he comes late."

I would be embarrassed, but Aditya was unfazed. When I asked Aditya why he did that, he would say, "I am only joking, but I also mean it actually". One day Chitra confronted Nanoo with his late return, and the next day, Aditya was taken to task by the gentle, good-hearted boss who knew he was being pranked by this young recruit. "You will create marital disharmony at my home. Young man, you better watch your step," Nanoo told him, his eyes twinkling. I don't think that ever stopped Aditya from continuing to tease Chitra about her husband.

While our stay at the bank's apartment was really pleasant, Aditya and I wanted a house of our own. "We must have our own piece of real estate in the city," he said, one day. It was an audacious desire, given the size of our pay packets, but that did not deter him. Dream big, work hard—that has been his way of life for as long as I have known him.

We began putting the money together and then, one day, we got a call from a broker saying that he had found the perfect house within our budget. We had to move fast. You know how it is in Mumbai, houses and time wait for no one. But we were falling short by about Rs 20,000. The bulk of the payment was thanks to a loan from Citibank, at special rates for employees, but we had to fork out the remainder and this was a substantial amount for us at the time.

We put our heads together, trying to figure a way out when it struck me that we could sell my jewellery. "We won't sell the ones with intricate designs or the ones that we have inherited from our grandparents but the rest we can sell," I suggested. We were almost ready to do that, but my father put his foot down. He offered to lend us the money but Aditya refused. Right from the start, he had said that we would never dip into the savings of my father or his. We wanted to be financially independent.

We kept looking for ways to make up the shortfall but were running out of time. Aditya then approached his father, for a loan, not a bailout. "I will pay you interest and you treat it like a fixed deposit in the bank," he told my father-in-law. His father lent us the money and that is how Aditya and I bought our first home, in Bandra, a stone's throw away from my parents' home.

> "A man is but a product of his thoughts; what he thinks, he becomes."
>
> M K Gandhi

9

LOVE IS A YO-YO ON JUHU BEACH

OUR FIRST CHILD, AMIT, WAS BORN WITHIN A YEAR OF OUR marriage and we were both completely hands-on during the pregnancy. I was working at the time and it was quite difficult managing home and work in addition to coping with the many changes the body goes through at such times.

Aditya had to deal with my mood swings and cravings. He was constantly being sent out for ice cream or, rushing to get me ice to keep my nausea down. Some days, he would be so nervous because he just didn't know how to help me through the different stages of pregnancy. Truth be told, he has always been the one who panics when one of us falls ill. Even now, he cannot bear it if our children or our grandson is unwell. He will stay up all night, talk to doctors, google remedies and fret and fume until things are back on track.

So there we were, me pregnant for the first time and Aditya, a nervous husband, doing everything I demanded at all odd hours. One day when we went to visit my parents (we were there almost every weekend), my mother saw what he was going through. She took him aside and handed him a cold beer and said, "Sit down. Leave it to me." He was so relieved that he had no objection when they suggested we move in with them until the baby was born. I am sure my mother and sister were very amused to see this side of their son-in-law.

We were usually looking for things to do over the weekends and Juhu Beach was a favourite haunt. Juhu is a western suburb in Mumbai, it is actually a narrow strip of land that abuts the sea—every Mumbaikar's favourite hangout where people sit back and enjoy the sunset as much as the profusion of tangy snacks and ice-slushes known as *golas*. The suburb is also home to many of the city's movie stars.

Aditya and I loved the beach and we would often spend an entire evening soaking in the smell of the sea and watching the sun set on the city. One Sunday evening, quite close to my delivery date, as we made our way back from the beach, I saw a young boy selling brightly coloured rubber balls filled with water and attached to a rubber string. Called yo-yos, these were popular kids' toys at the time.

Aditya was amused but he bought me a few yo-yos, teasing me all the time about it though. I was due soon and he would happily indulge every wish of mine. The next day being a Monday, I remember Aditya going off to work early in the morning. Ritu and I decided to spend the morning at the salon. We both felt that once the baby arrived, I would have no time for myself and hence we should make the best of the opportunity at hand.

It turned out to be a very short visit, however. Barely a few minutes after we reached, the salon owner who knew us well, packed me up with a set of towels and called a taxi to take me home. "Get to the hospital as fast as you can, her water bag has burst," she told us.

Aditya was in a meeting when I called him. "My water bag has burst," I told him. He was livid. "What is wrong with you," he said. "I will buy you some more! You didn't have to call me out of a meeting just to tell me that the yo-yos have burst. Really, Smiley..."

For a moment I was taken aback. He would often scold me for behaving childishly but then it struck me. Aditya thought I was taking about the yo-yos! I nearly fell down on the floor laughing, so much so that it took me some time to tell him what the real story was.

He was instantly apologetic and nervous. A string of questions followed: Was I all right? How did I know I was going to deliver the baby soon? By then I could barely get a word in through my giggles, but managed to assure him that I was absolutely fine and that he should come to Breach Candy Hospital, where our doctor was waiting for us.

This is the story of how our first-born, our son Amit, came into our lives—soaked in laughter and love. That's how I see our life too—through our ups and downs, it is Aditya's sense of humour and ability to make a joke out of anything that has seen us through.

Sometimes, even situations that could have blown up into a serious row have dissolved into funny stories that we tell our children and friends. There is this story that I often remind Aditya about. It was the first time his father came to stay with us. Dad was very keen to visit his son and daughter-in-law in Mumbai. One fine day, he landed up home and announced he was going to stay with us for a while. On our first weekend together as we all sat down for lunch, I saw that my father-in-law was not eating anything. He sat quietly looking down at his empty plate, even though the table was quite full. I asked him, "Dad, what is the matter? Why aren't you eating anything?" At first, he didn't say anything and then very softly muttered, "I will eat when my food arrives."

I was then enlightened by my father-in-law that he was what we call a pure non-vegetarian! Unfortunately, that afternoon, the table held only vegetarian fare. Aditya had not warned me and neither had Kalam Singh. I was so embarrassed, but I convinced him to give up his non-vegetarian rule for one meal. And ever since, I made sure that no matter what the menu was, there would be enough non-vegetarian choices for my father-in-law. Aditya never stopped laughing about it, neither did his dad.

> "Laugh as much as possible, always laugh. It's the sweetest thing one can do for oneself & one's fellow human beings."
>
> Maya Angelou

10

SMALL TALK

AS AN AIR FORCE KID, ADITYA GREW UP IN ALMOST EVERY PART of the country. His childhood was a string of new schools, new friends, weekends at the clubs and parties at home. I, on the other hand, grew up in a protected environment. Both at home and my boarding school. At school in Ooty, I was used to a restricted life under the sharp eye of my tutors and home wardens and at home, my parents' word was final.

I don't remember venturing out much for parties and such. In fact, we hardly ever entertained at home. Aditya was used to a more social upbringing. Aditya's parents often had guests over and hosted many official parties, and then as a trainee in Citibank, he and his friends regularly hosted large get-togethers. In the early years of marriage, Aditya and I found ourselves being regularly invited to cocktail parties or dinner dos, especially over the weekends, with his colleagues from Citibank. I was a bit nervous about these parties, but I think Aditya was even more nervous about me at these parties.

I have always been quite outspoken, never really knew how

to indulge in small talk and never held back my opinion in a conversation. He would worry that I would say something I should not have, or that I didn't reply in an appropriate manner, or that I wasn't smiling enough... and so on. But he never said anything to me at the party; the moment we would get into the car, he would start pointing out what and where I had messed up, in his view. He would go on and on saying, "You should have said this or, you should have not said that."

I took it for a while and then I told him—"You have two options. One is that I stop coming with you for the parties. *Na rahegi baas, na bajegi bansuri*" (a Hindi proverb that means if you remove the cause, the effect is automatically taken care of.) The alternative was that once we enter a party, "I go one way and you go the other," I told him.

"You don't hear what I say, so you don't comment on it either," was my logic. He heard me out and we decided to go our separate ways at official parties ever since, because he wouldn't go without me. Since that party, Aditya hasn't really said anything about what I say or don't say at these large gatherings and over the years, I too learnt how to entertain and throw large parties at all our homes. These are rollicking affairs with an unending supply of food, drink and laughter—three ingredients for the good life in our household.

However, let me add that I did surprise him with my social skills once. Aditya was travelling for some assignment and he wanted me to attend a party being organised in honour of Lawrence (Larry) Small, the legendary CEO of Citibank at the time.

Everyone had been invited with their spouses. Since Aditya

was away on tour and would be meeting Mr. Small the next day in office, he wanted me to go to the party, even if it was for a short while. I was very reluctant. I hated places where I didn't know anyone. Without Aditya by my side, I knew I would be totally lost in the large gathering. But since he was so insistent, I promised him I would go there, show my face and disappear in an hour.

As the evening approached, I faced it with dread. But then a promise has to be kept. So off I went, said my hellos and found myself a dark corner where I sat quietly nursing my Coke. I thought I was camouflaged by the dark shadows of the evening and that soon, when everyone got busy with their drinks, I would disappear.

But as I was contemplating my exit, I saw this man striding towards me. He wasn't Indian, had a rather large frame that gave him a huge height advantage over me and had an extremely confident air about him. He came over and said, "You have found a quiet spot. Lucky you! May I join you?"

I didn't know who he was but he was an extremely interesting gentleman. He was full of stories and before I knew, an hour had flown by. We chatted about his love for the country—he had travelled across India on a sabbatical from Citibank. He told me he played the banjo and that he had often played it for strangers during his travels around the world. He loved Indian family values and, "Next life, I want to marry an Indian girl," he said.

I was fascinated by the stories and was curious about how he managed to get clothes his size, given his large frame. He explained that he bought two shirts and then had his tailor fix the sleeves for him. Finally, I had to leave as I had left Amit at home.

He asked me who my husband was and we shook hands and he introduced himself as Larry Small.

The next day, Aditya came back from work in the evening and stared at me open-mouthed. "What on earth did you talk to Larry Small about?!" I had no idea that I was talking to 'the' Mr. Small until the very end. But the rest of the people at the party had all been watching and they accosted Aditya the moment he went to work. Some were jealous and some were simply amused at my ability to keep the big boss engrossed in conversation for an hour. As for me, I was just happy that I had managed to attend a party that Aditya really wanted me to, without putting my foot in my mouth.

> "Simplicity is a difficult thing to achieve."
>
> Charlie Chaplin

11

LIFE IS AN AIRPORT CAROUSEL

AMIT WAS PERHAPS A YEAR OLD WHEN ADITYA AND I WENT TO Chandigarh for his *mundan*—the ceremony that accompanies a child's first haircut. It was a grand affair and there were close to 1,500 people who attended the ceremony, a much larger turnout than we had for our wedding.

Aditya's grandmother, a strong and feisty woman of an indeterminate age, had commandeered the whole operation. She refused to listen to anyone, even her troublesome grandson who had managed to get his way with a small wedding and a handful of guests. No way, she declared, was she going to do the same for her great grandson. She ignored Aditya's protests and invited almost the entire town for the ceremony.

I remember both of us panicking at the number of people walking up and pinching our son's cheeks or holding him up, all through the day. In our tiny apartment in Mumbai and our rather structured lives, we had been extremely wary about germs and infections and Aditya would insist that we all had to wash our hands with Dettol before we could go near Amit. In Chandigarh,

Aditya was politely told to keep his fetishes to himself. His grandmother had raised 11 children and could not care less about our new-age parenting rules.

Aditya's family home was sprawling. Full of aunts, uncles and cousins, I don't remember a dull moment in all our visits there. Amit was everybody's pet and everyone looked after him. We were used to looking after him all by ourselves in the city. It was a complete change of routine to have so many willing, helping hands to take care of him.

On one of our visits, one of his cousins told me about this beautiful cottage cum getaway near Simla called Wildflower Hall. It was a stunning property, wasn't owned by any of the five-star hotels at the time as it later came to be and was much recommended by all who had been there.

I convinced Aditya that we should escape for a night or two and let Amit be taken care of by his grandparents and aunts. Aditya is always up for travel; he enjoys going to new places and sampling the local food. Even now when we travel, he finds out everything interesting about the place before we get there. What to eat? Where is the best view? What are the best things to buy? He turns into a living encyclopaedia of the place.

To get back to our planned getaway to Wildflower Hall, Aditya was more than happy to slip away from Chandigarh for a few days. But he warned me that we would be travelling to a remote location and "Just in case," he said, "you start missing Amit and want to come back instantly, it won't be possible."

The place was like a slice of heaven on earth—greenery all around, sharp blue skies that we could stare at all day and nice and helpful staff. What more does one need on a holiday?

But as the hours went by, I was struck by this inexplicable mix of fear and longing in my heart. Still, I kept my misgivings to myself. The second day was tougher, but I was holding it together until the hotel set up a bonfire for us in the evening, and organised some local singers to belt out our favourite songs. That was it. I started sobbing, silently at first and then uncontrollably. Aditya was frantic. He couldn't understand what had gone wrong, had he made a mistake? Was there something bugging me? Finally, I told him, "I want to see Amit."

He looked at me like he had known this was coming. Wait another day, he said. It was already late evening and as he had said, there was no way to travel back to Chandigarh at that hour. I somehow lasted the night, but at the crack of dawn, I dragged him out of the hotel and took the first bus back home. And what do I see there? Amit was happily playing with his cousins with all his aunts and uncles fawning over him.

Aditya has never stopped reminding me about our holiday and my crying fit. But then he admits that it is this love for my children and our family that has made him a family man. Both of us have always made an effort to keep the communication lines open with the children and today, when I think of Amit settled in another country living his life with a family of his own, I blush at the memory of that night. We've come a long way, right!

Also, I have to add that both Aditya and I have travelled extensively, ever since. Some of it was for his work, as Citibank posted him at exotic new places but a lot of it was also on holiday. And there have been times that I have left our son Amit and our daughter Amrita behind with my sister, who was always ready to help out just so that I could be with Aditya. And I haven't cried.

I went on an all paid for world tour this one time because Citibank decided to reward Aditya for having surpassed his target many times over. We went to so many places. That was just the beginning of a life full of new places and new experiences. Over the next few years, we moved to Athens, then Al-Khobar in Saudi Arabia, followed by Hong Kong and Malaysia and many other cities. We also travelled extensively on holidays—dashing in and out of airports, exploring little known gems in Europe and Asia. The wheels had been firmly strapped to our feet. A new phase of our life began to take shape, one that would take us away from the familiar comfort zone of our routine lives.

> “Love does not claim possession,
> but gives freedom.”
>
> Rabindranath Tagore

12

AL-KHOBAR VIA ATHENS

"SEND ME TO SAUDI ARABIA," ADITYA SAID, NEARLY THROWING Victor Menezes, his boss and the country head of Citibank at the time, off his chair. Aditya's request had come after months of agonising and worrying about our future. Just as he had been sure that he wanted a small wedding, there was another thing he was absolutely determined about—we had to make it on our own. We would build a good life, but we would do it with our money.

Working with Citibank brought with it a sense of glamour and a lot of respect, but much of the salary disappeared in taxes. We were left with very little in hand and Aditya and I had spent hours talking into the night, budgeting for a secure future for our children and our parents.

When Aditya approached Victor, money was on his mind. He had done his homework. Citibank had a small operation in terms of the number of people employed in Saudi Arabia. but was large in terms of the revenue generated. So it had popped up as a lucrative idea. Salaries were tax exempt in the Middle East at the time as the kingdoms were going all out to attract the best talent to their shores. Three years (at the most) is what Aditya had planned for us to live there and make enough money and come back to India.

On paper the plan seemed perfect, but Victor threw a fit. He told Aditya that it was as good as signing the death warrant on his career. "You are a rising star. If you go, all your colleagues will be your bosses by the time you get back," he thundered. When that didn't work, he offered more perquisites—a better apartment, a new refrigerator and such other things. Aditya was unmoved. Victor had no idea, perhaps, of the determination of this young Citibanker. Once he had made up his mind, and unless you could rationally argue him out of it, he was not going to give up.

Aditya reassured Victor, "That's fine, I can soon outgrow them but I need the financial security." He was confident that he could make up for the lost years in terms of seniority as long as he had enough money in the bank. Victor finally relented. He signed off on a posting at Citibank, Al-Khobar, a port city that was built on the country's vast oil riches. It had a huge expatriate population, working for either Aramco or Citibank, but nothing else. Not only was it far away from the world we were familiar with, it seemed like it would be terribly dull and uninteresting—there weren't any entertainment avenues in terms of movie halls and such and there would be no friends and family around us either.

We knew what we were signing up for and, I was as committed as Aditya towards building a better future for ourselves. Amit was a toddler at the time, and many people told us that it would be difficult raising a child without help. But I was not afraid and neither was Aditya. Success is all about hard work, which as he keeps repeating, never harms anyone. So, when Victor told us about the new posting, we jumped at the offer.

However, there was a glitch. It was already close to the end of the financial year and it would take another six months for a visa to Saudi Arabia, as was the case at the time. Aditya wanted to begin the new financial year with a new and tax-exempt salary structure, this was critical if we had to keep to the schedule of our three-year plan for us.

People marvel at the focus with which Aditya has expanded the HDFC Bank or the passion with which he drove its quarterly earnings. But I am never surprised. He has always been this way; he sets a goal and never gives up.

A solution was worked out and Aditya was appointed as the head of the Citibank Al-Khobar office. While his visa was getting processed, he was asked to head to the training centre at Athens. We were to be given a per diem (a daily allowance) for living in Athens while Aditya's salary would be paid in Saudi Arabia (as he had wanted). It meant leaving immediately for Athens and then six months later, move to Al-Khobar.

We left almost overnight. Aditya and I landed up in Athens in this breathtakingly beautiful suburb called Glyfada where the training centre was located. Our service apartments came with the best amenities and the daily allowance more than covered our expenses.

It was here in Athens that I first understood the concept of and the joys associated with the term TGIF (Thank God it's Friday). At the Citibank centre, every Friday, lunch was a community affair. Work stopped by noon and all the wives would land up at the office for a simple sandwiches-and-salad lunch and then usually, Aditya would whisk us off for a weekend to an island or into the mountains.

Greece is a beautiful country and I don't think I could have had a better introduction to its paradisiacal islands than those carefree weekends that we spent touring them. It wasn't just us, but the entire Citibank team would be off over the weekend—our service apartments emptied out as people hit the road or jumped on to a boat and set about exploring the Greek countryside.

Aditya worked really hard and his work was noticed and appreciated by the people high up in Citibank, which made our stay even more enjoyable. Before we knew it, the six months were up and we were on our way to Al-Khobar.

> “The secret of getting ahead
> is getting started.”
>
> Mark Twain

13

COFFEE, WINE AND DESERT GAMES

ADITYA IS A GOURMET. AS HIS WIFE AND CO-TRAVELLER OF SO many years, I know that there is not a single local delicacy that he has not sampled in the numerous places that we have been to. And his list of places to eat in every city across the world is more authentic than anything you will find in a tour guidebook.

However, ask him to boil an egg or, pick up a ladle in the kitchen, and he is completely lost. He calls himself an 'executive' chef. One who has never stepped into the kitchen, but always wants to know what is on the menu and never fails to comment on the taste.

His trials in the kitchen have given us some truly funny moments. One that I remember very clearly, dates back to around 1981–82, and it took place in our home in Al-Khobar.

Soon after Athens, we had to come back to Mumbai for a month while the visa interviews were conducted and the embassy gave its final stamp of approval for our stay in Saudi Arabia. Once we reached there, I realised that the place was even more remote than I had imagined. If you were to go there today, it glitters like gold in the desert sun. But at that time, Al-Khobar was in the middle of nowhere.

Our house was located in a cluster of 10 villas, all occupied by Citbankers. It was in a large gated complex with a high wall fencing it off from the outside world. Our neighbours were from other parts of Asia, but we were the only Indians there. We spent most of our time with each other and except the odd shopping trip to the only big store in the city, I hardly ever ventured out of the complex.

All our villas looked alike—a small yard in front and similar furniture—we could barely distinguish one from the other. We were around the same age too, as were our children.

Coming back to the kitchen and Aditya. Those days, we had set a monthly routine for ourselves. On a Friday, which was the day off, all the families in the complex would have a meal together. We took turns hosting each other so that the burden of cooking and cleaning was shared among us all.

In my case, the menu was always fixed. It had to be a vegetarian meal and *rajma chawal* (kidney beans and rice) was a must. I would keep things ready a day before, cutting and chopping everything to minimise the work on that day, while Aditya took over the cleaning of the house. Our lunch would be followed by a few rounds of board games and coffee. On one such occasion, we had all sprawled over the carpets after a heavy lunch and when the time came for coffee, Aditya was put in charge of the task. I was told to relax as I had already spent too much time in the kitchen and had to manage six-month-old Amrita.

Everyone told him, "Aditya, you needn't worry. It is not much. Just put the kettle on and measure out a spoon of coffee in the mugs. We will simply pour out the water and stir in our own coffee." Aditya said, "Don't worry. What is the big deal in making coffee? It's just boiling water. How can anyone go wrong with that?" And off he went to the kitchen, and came back with a satisfied smile on his face.

Soon we all got engrossed in the game and coffee receded to the back of our minds. It was a while before one of us piped up and noticed that the kettle was taking unusually long to whistle. "Perhaps, Aditya has overfilled the kettle," someone said. "*Haan*(yes), maybe," we said, letting the stupor of the afternoon excuse our laziness. We continued playing.

But when a long time had passed and there was still no sign of the kettle singing, one of our friends went over to see what the problem was. He came back grinning. Aditya had diligently followed instructions. The kettle had been filled, the mugs were arranged in a row with a spoon of coffee and sugar in each—just as he had been told. But he had not lit the gas and as a result the kettle full of water was idling away on a cold burner while we waited for it to bubble. I don't think anyone ever trusted him to do anything else in the kitchen after that.

We spent two years in Al-Khobar, instead of the three years that we had planned. Our six-month stint in Athens had given us a head start and helped put aside the targeted amount well before time.

We were glad to be able to make our way back home but our time in Al-Khobar was precious. Aditya and I learnt a lot there—

from managing our children all by ourselves, to managing the challenges of operating an office in Saudi Arabia, to making wine at home—we did it all. We even bought our first Audi car in Al-Khobar. It was a deep shade of blue and the thrill of owning our first car bought with our money was so huge that I think nothing really could replace that—no matter how many big cars we may have owned, or countries we may have travelled to, thereafter.

Our years with Citibank have created lasting memories. Not just the many cities that we were posted in and the different people we met, but also the way the organisation looked after us. While we were at Al-Khobar, for instance, Citibank would offer us an all-expenses-paid holiday every three months to compensate for the hardship caused by working in a remote location. This is what initiated us into the world of travel, encouraging us to explore exotic places in Europe and Asia and exposing us to new cultures and cuisines. Citibank called these holidays 'Rest and Recreation' or 'R&R'. Even now, when we travel, be it in India or abroad, I always remember the trips we made in our early years when I was just about discovering a world away from home. And in that sense, Al-Khobar holds a special place in our hearts.

During my stay there, I would often hear people say that this was going to be the Paris of the East. I used to wonder, how would they ever manage to transform this dusty, bare town into a city of romance and light. There was so much construction work that it looked like someone had drilled holes all over its surface and forgotten to fill them up. Things have changed significantly now, they tell me.

> "When the mind is pure, joy follows like a shadow that never leaves."

Gautam Buddha

14

FLOWERS AND FENG-SHUI

IT TOOK ME AROUND FOUR HOURS TO TRAVEL TO SHIRDI, A famous temple town near Mumbai. Shirdi is the former home of a revered Indian sage who is known as Sai Baba and the temple dedicated to him is a major pilgrimage site in the country. It attracts lakhs of devotees from all over the world.

I decided to undertake the journey. The roads were bad and it was quite a journey, but I had to go. For this is what I had on my mind, all the way on my flight back to India from Dammam (the closest airport to Al-Khobar).

It was a short trip. Asking Ritu to look after Amit for a day, I took off. When I reached the temple, surprisingly there was barely any crowd. I went right in and sat down in front of the idol of Sai Baba. I have always had tremendous faith in His power and I began relaying my heart's desire—that which had dragged me all the way from Saudi Arabia to Shirdi—my eyes shut in prayer.

"Look," I said, "I will try for a child only if I get a daughter. Otherwise I am happy with my son. Please show me that you have received my prayer, give me a sign. Anything—anything at all, let a flower drop from your garland or... just let me know that you heard my prayer."

Believe it or not, a flower dropped. That's all I wanted. I returned to Mumbai and was quite sure that I would soon have a daughter. When I told Aditya, he was most amused at my confidence. But then, nine months later Amrita came into our lives, and our family became complete.

It was also time to head back to India. We had managed to save enough money, thanks to our short stint at Athens and the forced saving that it imposed upon us since our salary was being deposited in a bank in Saudi Arabia while we lived off a per-day allowance. Instead of the three years we had planned initially, we were able to move back in two. But it was not Mumbai that we came home to, we moved to Delhi.

With two young children and with Aditya's increasingly busy schedule, those years seem like a blur. But what I remember clearly is that living in Delhi with Aditya was like living inside a food museum. He wanted me to taste everything—dragging me to the place that made the best chicken to the place that served the softest naans. Kebabs at Jama Masjid to *keema kaleji* at ITO—I have tried them all. We must have also covered every chaat maker in town, such was his enthusiasm.

Aditya loves to eat and he also loves to feed others. He has taken his colleagues to restaurants they would otherwise have never stepped into, just to taste the perfect dal or the spiciest mutton curry. Years later, when he was with HDFC Bank, there is a story that Samir Bhatia, his friend and colleague, recalls with great relish.

One afternoon, Aditya sauntered up to Samir and a few others around lunch time and said, "*Chalo aaj main sab ko khana khilata hoon.*" (Lunch is on me, folks.) Everyone trooped into his car, a Maruti Esteem at the time, and those that didn't fit in, were asked to follow in a cab and meet them at Siddhi Vinayak temple—a temple dedicated to the Lord Ganapati and one of the most-visited shrines in the country. It is a well-known city landmark that attracts people from all over the world and is known for the long queues outside its gates every Tuesday, an auspicious day of worship for Ganapati, the god who removes all obstacles.

The expectation all around was that there must be a new five-star hotel in the area and they would be treated to a grand lunch. After all, the boss was taking them out! To their utter surprise, Aditya led them into this tiny room that had a large fan whirring in the corner and a few tables set out in a row. A few local workers and cab drivers in the typical khaki uniform were at the tables.

All eyes turned towards the group walking in, in well-cut suits and ties. Aditya sat down and without a word, rolled up his sleeves and ordered almost everything that was on the menu. It was a meal to remember, the taste of which lingers in their conversations even today.

There is a childlike honesty in Aditya. He loves to experience new things and also wants all his loved ones to be a part of his experiences. Soon after we got married, we went to Simla where he took me to meet his favourite *ghodawala* (a man who offers his horse for short rides to tourists), his school teachers and all the spots that he spent time in. In Delhi too, he would always introduce me to his favourite haunts.

Many of his colleagues in Citibank and HDFC talk about his simple tastes and his ability to talk the language of the people—a rustic charm that has set him apart from his peers. I believe that it is his large Punjabi heart that endears him to people. Even when he is playing a prank on them, they take it in their stride with a grin.

A close friend who has often been at the receiving end of his jokes was completely taken by surprise when on one of his birthday mornings he opened the door to find a gift-wrapped cauliflower from Aditya. The previous day, the two had been joking about birthday gifts and such other matters when Aditya promised to send him a flower he would never forget. Cauliflower, incidentally, is also known among the local vegetable sellers as 'flower'.

However, as much as he is the funny man at parties, he is also a hard-nosed professional. He can be extremely unforgiving and shrewd when it comes to running a business, but he does it with such panache that he has often won over his most strident critics and detractors with the way he has handled a delicate situation or defused a toxic one.

For instance, there was this one time we were in Hong Kong. Aditya was working closely with a team of Chinese traders who, it is well known, are very wary of outsiders. With Aditya, they had their guard up from the start. Aditya knew that he had to be careful and sensitive about the situation because when you are in another country, the cultural contracts are just as important as the professional ones.

One day, Aditya went over to their office to discuss a proposal and also went into the trading room. The Chinese traders didn't like anyone else stepping into the trading room and they let him know about it in no uncertain terms. The trading room is out of bounds for him, they told him. "Looks like it brought us bad feng shui, we lost money," said the person who was guiding Aditya around the place.

Aditya is the last person to come in the way of making money. But he knew that there was more to their objection than commerce. He also knew that the community of traders he was dealing with were bullies, but they backed off as soon as someone stronger bullied them back.

It was a tricky situation–new city and new people meant he had to tread carefully while he established his authority. He was also aware that his actions would reflect on the bank, which meant that he couldn't let personal ego or grudges come in the way of a professional relationship.

He decided that if he wasn't going to be allowed into their trading rooms, then he would not go to their office at all. But that didn't mean that work would come to a standstill. The traders would have to trudge half way across town to his office if they wanted their proposals cleared. This soon became quite troublesome and quietly without much of a fuss, Aditya was given free run of their office.

His approach has usually been direct, but constructive. A similar story played out in Malaysia, which was the last place that he was posted at for Citibank, before he left to set up HDFC Bank. When we moved there, many people had warned us about potential employee trouble. And sure enough, Aditya realised that it was quite a situation that he had inherited from his predecessor.

The local employees were unhappy and things were worse when they saw that they would have to report to an Indian CEO.

They sent a representative to meet Aditya with a long list of demands. Not willing to commit one way or another before he had spent some time with the issues raised, Aditya said, "Give me three months."

Eager to drive a hard bargain and under the impression that they could bully a new CEO, the employees said they were not sure that they could wait that long. Their tactic had worked in the past—several former CEOs had caved in to their demands when faced with the threat of an internal revolt. But Aditya, having dealt with similar tantrums in Hong Kong, was well prepared. In that case, he said, they could hand in their resignation letters and he would be happy to process them without delay.

With his blunt ultimatum Aditya won their respect and soon, their love too. When we left, his team threw a massive party for him (which is a story by itself) and many have become our lifelong friends.

> "Let us never negotiate out of fear,
> but let us never fear to negotiate."
>
> John F Kennedy

15

A TREE TOO FAR

AFTER RETURNING TO INDIA FROM SAUDI ARABIA, WITH TWO young children and elderly parents-in-law, I had my hands full. And Aditya's workload was also steadily increasing. The days were a blur; I don't think we had any time for ourselves those days. We were allotted a beautiful house called 'Shanti Niketan' in Delhi, but to our dismay we landed up to find that the house was caught in the middle of a huge family dispute and Citibank had to hurriedly find us accommodation elsewhere. Being Citibank, they always did things with great style, so we stayed at the Taj Palace Hotel for six months before moving into our home.

This has been a kind of pattern for us. When we moved to Mumbai, for instance, the house that the bank had allotted us wasn't ready. We stayed for three months at The President, as it was called then (now Taj Vivanta). After that too, we had to move two houses before finally moving into the Citibank apartment at Il Palazzo in Malabar Hill.

It was a nomadic existence. By the end of it all, I could pack up a home blind-folded. Sometimes, we would live out of boxes, not wanting to unpack fully because the next move was just a few months away. But there were a lot of benefits too—our houses were always large and in the best of locations. Our Il Palazzo home was a duplex apartment. Citibank CEOs were given the royal treatment—not just furnished houses, they were also given generous allowances for redoing the homes. From crockery to furnishings, we would get the best of everything.

In all of this continuous shifting of homes and the uncertainty of new cities and schools and such other matters, there was one ritual that Aditya never let go. We always set aside time for a holiday, no matter how busy he was.

One summer when we were staying in Delhi, we managed quite a long vacation. We took a three-week break in Manali.

There weren't as many hotels back then in Manali and it was still not the popular destination that it has become today. Through a friend, I think, we heard about these old houses being rented out as vacation homes and we decided to book two. We were a big family—the four of us and Aditya's parents, and it was decided that we would all go, even take our helpers and attendants along.

The cottages were quite bare, but they came with a kitchen and some basic furniture. We had to carry our own cooking utensils and implements along with vegetables and masalas. As you can imagine, it was quite an adventure. But I am happy to say that we were quite an enthusiastic couple and we managed to transport everything and everyone without much incident.

It was a lovely place. The bungalows were quaint with an old-world charm and it was quite a relief to be away from the heat and dust of Delhi. Besides, we were pleasantly surprised to find that some of our friends had the same idea as us and were booked in similar bungalows around us! That was a big bonus. We hadn't expected any friends and their company made our stay even more enjoyable.

One lovely, sunny morning, it was decided we would all go on a picnic. Off we went with a packed hamper and a bag with some *chatai*s (mats) and napkins. Aditya's parents were with us too and they stopped mid-way through our trek, settling in a spot where they could soak in the morning sun. We walked on, looking for a comfortable spot to flop down and found a tree that generously spread its branches to create a shaded spot that looked just perfect for a lazy day outdoors. There were six of us, three couples, all friends from Delhi and we quickly set out everything—the *chatai*s, food and poured out some tea from the flasks. Why waste even a minute, when the day was so beautiful, right?

But, one of us suddenly pointed out another tree, a short distance ahead that seemed to be even larger and shadier, besides offering a stunning view of the valley. Let's move up a bit, he suggested. We were all quite keen but I took one look at Aditya and I knew this was not going to happen. He lay there quietly, staring up at the sky with a half-smile. On a holiday, he wants to do as little as possible, contrary to the image of a man in a hurry that he has in the professional arena.

No one believes me when I tell them that he is a 'do nothing' kind of a person at home. At work, however, he is like an unstoppable roadroller, taking everyone with him, making the most out of every moment. But believe me, when he is not working, he is a completely different person.

I wondered what excuse Aditya would make to get out of the new plan. Our friends were all keen and they were about to pick everything up and move to the other spot. Aditya looked at the tree and went into deep thought and then flopped on his back and said, "*Nahin yaar* (no yaar), that's a tree too far." We burst out laughing—you can't call him lazy or get irritated with him, even when he gets his way.

However, I have to make a clarification here that even on a holiday, if Aditya sees something that he thinks will find a home in our house, he will move heaven and earth to get it. Our home in many ways is like a quilt of stories–each object is a memory of another place and another time. From the furniture to the lights and the door, we have picked them up on our travels, often going to great lengths to bring them home. Aditya stops at nothing—I remember we were coming back from Prague, our luggage was all packed and there was no space to squeeze anything else in when we saw a beautiful chandelier. Aditya and I fell in love with it and he made sure that we packed it all up, even when we were running out of time. He carried the heavy box and ran to the boarding gate, as they were making the last calls by then. The same man who will make every excuse he can to not move a few paces because he would rather lie on his back will also overturn every hurdle in his path to get what he wants—this is his abiding trait, be it at home or at work.

"Arise, awake and stop not,
until the goal is achieved."

Katha Upanishad

16

NEVER A DULL MOMENT

WE SAT AROUND A TABLE FULL OF PEOPLE AT A HOTEL IN Jakarta while everyone congratulated us. Aditya had just been promoted at Citibank and his star was rising, as they say, within the bank. I was quiet, nibbling my food while taking in some of the advice I had received from our friends and family, ever since they heard about Aditya's new role in the bank. They suggested that I should start entertaining more as the top bosses would expect regular dinner parties and that senior dignitaries from all over the world would visit our home.

There were so many people giving me so much advice that I was confused and extremely worried. I wasn't one for large parties at the time (although much has changed over the years). Ever since the news of his promotion had become official, panic gripped me. I was afraid that I would make some mistake, or fail to live up to the expectations of the bosses and that would reflect badly on Aditya.

Finally, Aditya asked me, "*Matam kyun mana rahi hai* (Why are you mourning)? I have been promoted!" I told him all my fears and he laughed and said, "Don't worry, the day is not yet here when I have to climb on your shoulders to rise in the bank."

A few days later we were at lunch and I found myself sitting next to Rana Talwar, a well-known banker and close friend. Our families go back a long way and he and Aditya had known each other from their days in Chandigarh. I asked him, "I am told that all these foreign banks expect the wives to organise these really fancy dinner parties and all that. Will I also have to do the same to keep the bosses happy?" He laughed and replied, "*Iska* career *buland hai*(His career is safe), with or without you." His words came as a huge relief and have over the years, proven to be absolutely right.

Aditya was a young CEO. Since he was working with a global bank, I had to quickly take on a role that was well beyond my years. I learnt how to adapt to different cultures and the varied expectations of people around him. But I never really tried to become someone I wasn't. And there have been times that this has worked in our favour too, much to our surprise.

We were posted in India at the time; there was this lady who shall remain unnamed, who would often accompany her husband, one of Citibank's top bosses, to India. We struck up a warm relationship and she would seek me out on all her trips. "I like being with you," she said. "You don't go out of your way to impress me and that makes it so easy."

Honestly, keeping one's bearings straight and not getting lost in the corporate rat race can be quite a challenge. I won't say it has always been smooth sailing, but it has been hugely entertaining and full of memorable moments and thrills.

Many of our experiences are now anecdotes that Aditya

regularly uses to drive home a point—with his family, inside the boardroom and even while enjoying a drink with friends.

One thing that he often says and that which cracks a smile in even most dour gentlemen is, "Does the gharial(crocodile) know?" Let me tell you the story behind this.

We had returned to India and were posted in Delhi. Aditya had just closed a very important deal for his bank with Scandinavian Airlines (SAS). It came through after weeks of negotiations and at the end of it all, the SAS CEO expressed his desire to visit Corbett Park, this one resort in particular that he had heard a lot about that was very remotely located and rustic. It didn't even have electricity.

Citibank organised the entire trip because everyone was very happy with the way the negotiations had worked out and we landed up at this resort–the CEO, his wife and three sons with Aditya and me. We spent a lovely weekend together and on the last day, the guide arranged for a fishing trip for Aditya and the CEO. The two of them were sitting quietly in the middle of the river, their fishing lines in water when there was a sudden flash in the water.

Aditya spotted the scaly body of a crocodile swimming towards them. "Let's get out," he said, pointing the creature out to the guide. It didn't bother the guide much, who told Aditya that he should not worry because it was just a gharial. "What do you mean?" Aditya asked him, his patience beginning to wear thin.

"Gharials are vegetarian," the guide told him. Aditya looked him in the eye and said, "Look, you know the gharial is vegetarian, I know he is vegetarian but does the gharial know he is vegetarian?" The guide immediately turned the boat around, laughing all the way back to shore.

This story has now become a standard line in our lives. Ask any of his friends and his colleagues at the bank and they all groan whenever this is mentioned. Because Aditya now substitutes the gharial in the joke with whatever else is the need of the hour. At the bank, for example, he would often talk his team out of some really far-out propositions by saying, "Look, I know you are doing this. You know you are doing this. But does the customer know that you are doing this?"

There is another story that we often talk about, not because it is funny, but because it showed us just how little we know about the world we live in. This is from one of our trips to Brazil. We were there for the World Cup and Aditya had an evening free. We decided to take a helicopter trip around the city. It was one of the routine 45-minute rides with a view of the beaches and the statue of Christ the Redeemer and the famed favelas. The pilot was a very friendly person and he was regaling us with stories about the city and the people and we urged him to go a bit lower than usual, just for a closer look at the tiny homes that looked like rows of colourful ants from above. He did so, only to zip back up in an instant as the helicopter was attacked by a stream of bullets! The people whose homes we had been looking at were extremely angry and for some reason saw all of us tourists as unwanted outsiders. This was their form of protest. It was a close shave for us and our pilot made a swift turn to take us back up into a safe zone—but it was quite a dramatic introduction to a beautiful country full of colour, exotic food and of course, football. I guess, c'est la vie!

“There is nothing in the world
so irresistibly contagious as laughter
and good humour.”

Charles Dickens
A Christmas Carol

17

A THANKFUL HEART

WHEN ADITYA WAS ABOUT TO JOIN CITIBANK, ONE OF HIS former colleagues tried to dissuade him. He asked him to reconsider saying, "Are you an accountant or a banker?" All this didn't matter to Aditya who simply wanted a better life (and a shorter commute). Citibank offered him a better salary, better house and a chance at a secure future. Plus, it meant that he would not have to travel all the way from Churchgate to Kandivali, almost two ends of the city.

More importantly, I think, he saw an opportunity and was confident that he could make the most of it. That is how he has led his life—be it within Citibank, or when he moved back to India to set up HDFC Bank, or as he expanded its scope to make it one of the best and most respected brands in the world today.

However, there is one story about his days as a student, when he was appearing for the chartered accountancy exams and living with his parents in Delhi that he tells with great relish. At the time, he too was very jittery about his future.

Aditya was studying to be a chartered accountant (CA) and those days he says, he hardly had time for anything else. He was hardworking, determined to clear his exams in the first attempt and with high grades because he knew how competitive the job market was. Aditya worked hard because as his dear friend and cousin, Uday Khanna says, he had something to prove.

Uday and Aditya, both had fathers in the armed forces and they attended their final years of school at Bishops School, Pune. Both fared poorly in their board exams and their parents had been extremely disappointed with the results. Uday jokes that it is because of the early shock and disappointment they had brought upon their parents that they both worked doubly hard to build a successful career for themselves.

Whatever the reason, Aditya was very worried about his employment prospects after completing the CA programme. He saw some of his batchmates strutting around confidently because they had been assured jobs with their father's accountancy firm or had a family friend who had promised them a position in his company. Aditya neither had his father's company, nor a family benefactor to fall back on.

He regularly complained to his mother (Kaushalya Puri) about their lack of connections. "My friends will be taken in with open arms into their jobs but what about me? Who do you know? When I finish, I will be finished," he would grumble.

His mother took it for a while and then she told him to stop worrying so much. She said, "How do you know I don't know anyone in high places? Wait till you graduate and then you come to me. Then we shall see who has high contacts and who doesn't. Believe me, I have the highest of them all."

This stopped him from complaining for a few months. But sure enough, when the results were declared, Aditya had done very well. He came back to her and said that it was time to activate those contacts. "I need a job and by the way, who is this contact of yours?" he asked his mother.

His mother looked skywards and pointing to the heavens said that she would put a good word in for him with her contact—god. After all, is there a bigger connection than him? Aditya didn't know what to say to his mother, except roll his eyes and grin.

Truth be told, Aditya didn't really need any contacts. His results were good and his friends from those days still talk about his phenomenal memory that helped him do extremely well in his final exams. He was able to find an opening at a big company soon enough and then move to Mumbai. After that, the world was his oyster. He moved to Greece, then to Saudi Arabia and then we lived all over Asia—Hong Kong, Singapore and finally Malaysia which was our last post with Citibank. There has been no reason to complain, except say our prayers and thank the heavens for his mother's deep connection with the highest authority of all.

> "Opportunity follows struggle.
> It follows effort. It follows hard work.
> It doesn't come before."
>
> Shelby Steele

Banker on the rise

03

18

HOME IS WHERE THE HEART IS

WE MOVED SO MANY HOMES WITH CITIBANK THAT I HAD begun to dread the next posting. Packing, unpacking and then settling into a new city—all of that was a big chore. But my irritation would melt in seconds, when I stepped into the homes that the bank offered us. If there is one thing that Citibank knew, it was to treat its employees with style.

In Hong Kong, we lived in an apartment at the plush Garden Terraces that belonged to the famed billionaire businessman, Stanley Ho. The view was spectacular—the Hong Kong skyline glittered and glowed outside my window like someone had plucked all the stars out of the night sky and put them up for a show. Even the house was stunning, spacious and fit for a king.

In Kuala Lumpur, Malaysia, where we were posted between 1992 and 1994, we lived in the swish enclave of U-Thant. It is one of the most expensive pieces of real estate in the country and this is also where all the consulates are located. We lived in an old colonial style bungalow, spread out over an acre and a half, which came with its own private pool and volleyball court.

Over the many years that he had spent, moving to different countries, Aditya had built up a reputation of sorts. He was seen as a hard-nosed worker who knew how to extract the maximum out of every deal and team. By the time we moved to Kuala Lumpur, his stock within Citibank was rising. The then CEO, John Shepard Reed, had Aditya pegged as one of the top 50 stars in the bank. As his responsibilities within the bank grew manifold, his influence also multiplied.

At home however, Aditya was the same person who had insisted on a small wedding—simple, always ready for a good laugh and focused on creating a safety net for his family. We were always careful with our money. Even today, Aditya does not believe in extravagance for his personal needs. He goes to a local barber for a haircut, does not bother with branded clothes and although he is always happy to spend on his children and for me, he thinks a million times before splurging on himself.

We were in Malaysia for two-and-a-half years and Aditya's parents would visit us often, spending months with us. Their health was failing by that time and they needed a lot of care and attention. I remember his mother telling me, "Smiley, *main apna* passport *gooma doongi toh* (I will deliberately misplace my passport) I can stay with you always."

Her innocence was touching but we also knew that our parents were growing old and we would soon have to find a way to come back to India to be able to look after them. However, there seemed to be little chance of that at the time since Citibank had mapped out a completely different trajectory for Aditya and we weren't complaining.

In the midst of all this, Aditya got a call one day from

Deepak Parekh, the chairman of Housing Finance Development Corporation. He was coming to Kuala Lumpur, he said, and invited himself over for a drink. We were only too happy to host him and even happier to discover that our old friend Bharat Shah, (currently the chairman of HDFC Securities) was working with UBS in Singapore at the time would also join us.

The evening was warm and we sat in the open, near the swimming pool where I ensured a continuous supply of food and drink. I could see the conversation getting really heated. I went over. Bharat quickly filled me in and I remember my first reaction was one of shock. "What! You two will run a bank!" We all had a good laugh but I saw that Deepak Parekh was very serious and he was telling Aditya that it was time to come home. He said he could not match the salary, but he was offering him the thrill of setting up an institution for his country and stock options.

It was a big decision to make. On one hand, Kuala Lumpur offered us the best of both worlds. We were well looked after, had a close set of friends and there were always some family members visiting. Amrita had settled in and was studying at the American School while Amit was in India at Mayo College. Plus, there was a constant flurry of activity.

We played host to an enviable cast of global dignitaries—I remember clearly the day Margaret Thatcher came home. She was hosted by Citibank. As she walked in with a large retinue, she stopped and admired the house, took time to talk to all of us and spent quite a lot of time just chatting with all the people who had come to see her. Shaukat Aziz, who went on to become the prime minister of Pakistan, was a guest too. Festivals were a community affair—on Diwali for instance, all through the day, people would walk in and out and the tables never ran dry of food or drink. It was called an 'open house' in Citibank parlance.

But there was another side to the story. Aditya's father's health was deteriorating and he had told us that he wanted to spend his last days with us. We had also been discussing going back intermittently as Aditya always wanted to do something for his country and look after his parents who, he knew, needed him more than ever before.

When the HDFC Bank offer materialised, perhaps fate was playing its hand once again in our lives. The risk was obvious, but so was the sense of duty and the thrill of setting up a new institution. Making a choice is never easy and this one was tougher than most.

I must add, it had been Aditya's longstanding desire to set up a bank of international standards and global repute in India. He would always tell me, "One day I am going to make a world-class bank for India, in India, for Indians."

His paternal grandmother (or *dadi*) was among his biggest supporters and she would always say, "*Beta*, India *ke liye badi batein kiya karo kyunki jangle mein mor nacha kisne dekha*." (Speak and do things that make people notice India's greatness otherwise it will be like the the peacock dancing in the jungle—magnificent but unnoticed.) She had great faith in her grandson.

Still, it was a tough decision. Aditya thought about it long and hard and then one evening, he sat me down and asked, "Smiley, what should I do?" I told him to follow his heart, I knew he would always take the right call. When he finally gave the 'all clear' signal to HDFC Bank, I was only too happy to come back to Mumbai, the city I had lost my heart to, a long time ago.

"Keep your fears to yourself,
but share your courage with others."

R L Stevenson

19

GOODBYE KUALA LUMPUR, HELLO MUMBAI

THERE IS A STORY THAT ADITYA'S CLOSE ASSOCIATE OF MANY years, Vipul Mehta, relates often and I am going to borrow that here. Vipul is Head of Asia Investments Singapore with Nomura Asset Management. He says that at one of the many investor conferences that he was a part of, Aditya was his usual self, cracking jokes and talking to everyone about the bank when he asked Vipul, "*Accha bata, gaadi mein* brake *kyon hoti hain*?(Tell me, why do cars have brakes?)" You must know that whenever Aditya asks a question like this, he has some answer up his sleeve. The question is only a ploy for him to have a good laugh at the other person's expense.

It was Vipul's turn to get his leg pulled and so he answered, "To bring it to a halt in time." Aditya immediately said in a booming voice, "*Kab tu kuch samjhega? Gaadi mein* brake *isliye hain taki hum usko full speed mein chala sake!*(When will you ever understand anything? We have brakes only so that we can drive our cars at full speed!)" He added, "My risk measures are my brakes. I put them in so that I can go full throttle without an accident."

This is how Aditya has been with most of the challenges that have come our way. He does not hesitate to take risks, only because he has factored them in. But I am happy to tell you this story where I, not he, was the brake that kept him safe.

Our days at Citibank were coming to a close because Aditya, after several meetings and trips to Mumbai and elsewhere, had finally said yes to HDFC Bank. It hadn't been all smooth sailing however; he had had several meetings with Deepak Parekh and with Deepak Satwalekar who was the managing director of HDFC at the time over the name of the bank. At one point, the discussion got really heated with them refusing to lend the HDFC brand name to the bank—one option was Bank of Bombay as Parekh had suggested and another was Bombay International as Satwalekar proposed. Aditya was very clear that he wanted the name HDFC for the bank. He made a statement to stay back in Kuala Lumpur and withdraw his resignation with Citibank if he didn't get his way. It was only after they reassured him that the bank would get the HDFC brand, did he finally commit to the task.

Meanwhile, a huge farewell party had been organised for Aditya by his colleagues in Kuala Lumpur. I was told by many that this is usually an all-night affair and that it involved a lot of singing, dancing and drinking, and then everyone would just grin and wink, expecting me to understand everything.

To tell you the truth, I did have some idea about what they were hinting at. Aditya's secretary had warned me that these parties could get really wild and that I should keep an eye out.

Before I say anything further, I want to add that the time and culture I am talking about here is very different from the one we are in today. Every society has its own social mores and practices and I have no problem with that at all.

To get back to the party, it was truly a wild one. There was a lot of dancing, I don't know how many people came up to us and recounted personal stories about Aditya. We had a lovely time, but as the night wore on, I got tired. The party did not show any signs of winding down. After some time, some of Aditya's team members noticed my sleepy state and said, "Smiley, you go home. Let Aditya stay back. See, he is having such a good time. We'll take care of him," they said. There was a room in the hotel that had been booked for him and he would spend the night there, or that was their plan. I don't know what came over me, but I saw a room key placed next to him and all those broad hints that people had been dropping my way, suddenly hit me.

I just stood there and held his hand and said, "I am sorry but my husband is coming back with me." They were all taken by surprise. "I am not going alone," I said, "Where I come from, a husband and wife leave together after a party." I simply led him out of the swanky five-star hall, where the party was organised, without so much as a word. He still laughs about it, telling me that I ruined his chances of a good time that night. That night, he was really thankful that I had been so firm about leaving together. I had put the brakes on at the right time!

When we were packing up in Kuala Lumpur, Aditya sent me and Amrita ahead so that we could settle in with the new school and home. Amrita had enrolled in the Bombay Scottish School, which was quite near the apartment that the HDFC team had given us in a building called Concord in Bandra. Aditya would join us a few months later. His secretary, Polly, told me not to worry about anything as she would take good care of 'boss'. Polly was like a mother figure in our lives. She always looked out for me and taught me so much about the local customs, food habits and other things that I will always be grateful to her.

"Smiley," Polly said, "You go ahead and set up the house. I will make sure that everything is running smoothly here and don't worry, I will make sure that he is not with the same woman every day. There will be a different woman in the house every day!" Of course, Polly was pulling my leg but I just wanted to be very sure and said, "No, no. Where I am from, one woman or many women, everything is a problem."

Polly and I had a good laugh and she said, "Smiley, why do you worry so much? Aditya will not do anything without you." Polly told me that many households accepted some degree of infidelity from their husbands as part of a healthy marriage. But that was never acceptable to me and I would tell her that nothing and no one comes between Aditya and me in this life. She would call me every evening to report back on Aditya and ask how I was coping with setting up a new home, back in Mumbai.

All these stories are like little pieces of coloured glass that reflect our life together, glued together by laughter, emotion and a lot of teasing and easy banter (as we say, *nok-jhok*). Aditya, as is his habit jokes about everything, even about us growing old together.

He says, "Smiley and me are like the proverb about an old king and his hookah. The king had nothing left, except his fraying royal robes and the fire in the hookah had long died down and its embers grown cold. But the king keeps on smoking. *Aag toh kab ki bujh gayi hai, ham hi hain jo wahi hookah gudguda rahen hain*. (The fire is long gone but we are still blowing down the cold hookah)." This, according to my husband, is the story of our lives today.

Laughter has kept our home fires burning. I don't know what I would have done if we didn't see the funny side of things. I am not sure I would have survived the first few months after moving back to Mumbai when I walked into a dirty, poky apartment that looked nothing like the sprawling house I had left behind in Kuala Lumpur. There was hardly any help, Amrita had a new school to adjust to and the house was full of cockroaches and stains. Where I once had a retinue of maids and attendants, there was hardly anyone to help me with the daily chores. However, soon enough, through the dark clouds that were gathering over our heads, we found a way to let the sunshine back into our lives.

> "Don't let the noise of others' opinions drown out your own inner voice."
>
> Steve Jobs

20

DOING IT OURSELVES

LOUD MUSIC GREETED ADITYA AS HE WALKED INTO MY SISTER'S house where Amrita and I had been staying since moving back from Kuala Lumpur. Our home was getting ready and I used to spend almost the entire day overseeing the work, cleaning up and setting the house in order. My sister's house was not only conveniently located, but also a place of great comfort, as we adjusted to the ways of the city and a new life.

Aditya walked in to see Amrita grooving to the hit song of the year '*Tu cheez badi hai mast mast*' (from the film *Mohra* that had just been released with Bollywood stars Raveena Tandon and Akshay Kumar). He had been really apprehensive about the move and we had spent hours discussing the impact on Amrita whose life was going to be turned upside down—from making new friends and going to a new school, she would also have to give up many of the luxuries that we had got used to in Kuala Lumpur. As for Amit, he was already in India, studying at the Mayo College in Ajmer and for him, it would have been less of an upheaval. That day, when Aditya saw Amrita jiving and dancing and singing with such abandon, he grinned and said, "She'll be all right."

Soon Aditya packed his bags and joined us in Mumbai and Concord, tucked away in a quiet corner in Bandra, became our home. He officially took charge in September 1994, joining the HDFC office at Sandoz House. It was a far cry from the swanky Citibank workspaces that he was used to. Broken chairs, half-done furniture, makeshift partitions—that's what his office looked like—not just for Aditya, but for all the people from Bank of America, Merrill Lynch, Reserve Bank of India that he was trying to get on board. Everyone was coming into an office that was nothing like the places they had worked in earlier. Everyone knew that they were all buying into a dream that could take off or fail. And fortunately, everyone was united by a common vision. But it was a really hard battle every day.

On the family front, I could see the toll it was taking on Aditya. Every day was a new challenge. There was this time he met some potential investors who could not even pronounce the name of the bank. Another time he went to meet a senior industrialist who kept him waiting for over half a day. After being considered among the top performers at Citibank, he was being dismissed as a flash-in-the-pan. That hurt, as did the huge adjustments that we had to make on the home front—be it the tiny living space after the sprawling home we had in Kuala Lumpur or some of the basic comforts that we had taken for granted at Citibank.

There was also a lot of self-doubt. Would he be able to deliver or would it all come crashing down like a house on fire? Would he be able to convince the best people to join and then stay with the bank? And the one question that he asked me over and over again: "Smiley, have we made a mistake?" But we could not show any of this to the world outside.

The worst days would be when one of his ex-colleagues from Citibank would call him. Their conversation would invariably turn to all the things that he had given up to come to Mumbai. And my task would become a hundred times more difficult. Years later, I asked him about the early years that took such a toll on all of us. Was it that he had underestimated the challenge of setting up a bank in India? Or was his confidence shaken by the number of hurdles that came his way?

"Neither," he said. There was never any doubt in his mind about the opportunity or the expertise of the team. "The implementation was going to be tough but if we did it right, we could create history," Aditya said. No country can move ahead with just public sector banks and foreign banks. You needed large private sector banks. All the indecision, anxiety and gloom—it was not about the opportunity or his capability and that of the people around him, but whether he was right to leave a cushy job and come to India.

Those were the doubts weighing heavy on his mind as he went to work, met clients and worked out a way to keep our family life stable and comfortable. Every day, when he came back from work, I sat with him for an hour or more, just talking to him and boosting his confidence. I found my own little ways to keep myself sane and happy too. It was not as if his work was the only thing that we had to deal with at the time. His parents were ill.

And Amrita was having a tough time at school, so my hands were full.

But it was also an exciting time. Just as Aditya was getting to know the new system and the new norms of banking, the bank and its team were also getting to know him. Very soon, word went around that if you were going out with the boss, you had to carry a wallet, because he never carried one. Even now, I keep the money when we go out.

Another practice that soon became an Aditya trademark was his fixation with punctuality—he never wears a watch but he is never late. His team knew that the worst start to a morning was when the boss saw you slip in late. He would make life miserable for those who missed their meeting schedules or didn't clock in on time, even if it were just a few minutes.

Aditya also never carries a phone. It used to irritate me no end, because I was never able to get a hold of him when I wanted to. But nothing I did would convince him to carry one, until one day, I bought him a phone. Do it for me, I told him.

He took the phone without a murmur and regularly carried it to office too. But what did he do with it? At some point in the day, he would dial my number and if, for any reason, I didn't pick up, he would switch it off and stuff it into the safe in his room. After that, the only time the phone came back into his hand was when he left for home. Neither could I return his calls, nor could I call him when I wanted to.

"Why do you never answer my calls?" I asked him. His answer: "Smiley how can I answer it? It is inside my safe." Why did he keep it in his safe? Because it was a gift of high value and he didn't want to risk losing it! I gave up and till this day, he is absolutely fine without a mobile phone.

Aditya is a careful spender. Actually, we both are and even today, an expensive gift is treasured like gold. Over the years, I won't deny that I have developed some expensive tastes, but not Aditya. He barely possesses any branded clothes and watches.

The good thing is that he does not insist that we all behave like him. He has grown used to the small extravagances that we indulge in, but perhaps that is a lesson he has had to learn the hard way, from his daughter.

It was a few years since we had moved to Mumbai and the bank was growing steadily. Our lifestyle had also changed as Aditya was doing well and he thought that this was the right time to instil a sense of value in Amrita. He began telling her stories about his growing up years. Calling her to his side, he said, "You know, you kids keep complaining about the AC not working and so on, but do you know that when I was in college, we didn't even have a music system and we listened to the 'Binaca Geet Mala' on radio. To keep ourselves cool we splashed water on the floor and then we switched on the fan."

Amrita heard him without saying a word and when he had finished, she said, "Papa, if you are missing all this so much then I will happily take them all out of your room. I will take out the AC, get you a radio and throw water on the floor. Right away." A wicked grin played on her face as we both burst out laughing.

> “Optimism is the faith that leads to achievement. Nothing can be done without hope and confidence.”

Helen Keller

21

A GIFT FROM THE OCEAN

ADITYA AND I WERE WALKING ALONG THE BEACH. WE HAD come away for the weekend with a couple of friends to Marve Beach where HDFC Bank has a holiday home. Barely over an hour's drive from the city, this place has been a favourite and easy getaway for us.

That morning, our friends were sleeping in late, but as was our habit, we were out early morning. The beach was empty except a few local boys drying the fishing nets and some stray dogs scampering across the sand. We were strolling, quietly taking in the sights and smells, when something caught my eye.

We walked closer and I saw this beautiful old tree trunk with gnarled branches. It lay on the beach, basking in the early morning sun. Such a beauty, I pointed it out to Aditya, telling him that it would have been really nice if we could make something of this. He nodded vaguely, not saying much.

The sun had just broken through the morning sky and as we walked up and down the beach, I threw many admiring glances at the tree trunk that glistened in the glow of the morning light.

We headed back home for breakfast, but as we stepped indoors, Aditya excused himself. Our friends were already at the table and he told them to get started. He would be back in a minute, he said. Some urgent work that couldn't wait, he mumbled.

He was gone for three hours. We were all worried sick, wondering what was keeping him so long. Finally, I saw him trudging back up the beach, but he wasn't alone. There was a large crowd around him and my first thought was that maybe, something had gone wrong. Why was Aditya being followed by so many people? But as they came closer, I saw that the people were carrying the tree trunk that I had admired and that he seemed to have barely noticed. I could hardly believe my eyes!

"Here Smiley, look what I have for you," he said, setting the trunk down on the patch of green in front of the house. How did he manage that? Aditya had gone back to the beach and found a few young men from the village nearby hanging around the tree trunk. He asked them if the trunk belonged to anyone. They had no clue, but said that the sea had thrown it up sometime during the night. They agreed to help him carry the trunk to the bungalow for a fee, and then everyone waited for the tide to come in so that the trunk could be pushed closer to land. Then, they had picked it up and brought it home.

I was taken completely by surprise. Here I was merely admiring the trunk, wishing I could use it somehow in our home and he had gone ahead and brought it in. That is how Aditya is. Nowadays I hesitate to point out things that are beautiful, or would look good in our home, simply because I am afraid that I will be sucked into a chain of events that I will have no control over.

Anyway, now we had this gorgeous piece of a tree in our possession and we had to find a way to use it. An architect friend agreed to come and take a look. He was stunned to see the piece—this is no ordinary driftwood, he told us, adding that usually tree trunks like this are picked up by sea pirates and sold for close to Rs 5 lakhs or even more. He traced the tree's origins to Africa and said that the knotty, gnarly part of the trunk was what is called a burl—a tree growth that forms out of a deformed seed—considered to be extremely sturdy and particularly suited for furniture making.

This huge piece of wood now resting in front of the house at Marve Beach had quite a journey before reaching us. We felt that it was only right that we give it a good home. "But how are you going to transport this into town?" a friend of ours asked, voicing our own apprehensions.

We had to have the tree trunk cut into manageable pieces, but without damaging the wood or its natural shape. An even bigger challenge was to find something or someone who would be able to slice through the log of wood. This turned out to be an almost impossible task, because this piece of wood was more like a lump of iron. Seasoned by the salty ocean water and sunlight, the tree trunk was impenetrable. Even the toughest axe that our carpenters brought turned out to be too weak for the job.

Finally, an electric cutter managed to break through and carve out six to seven pieces. Aditya made sure that we didn't lose the natural curve of the trunk and the cuts were along existing lines, so that the beauty that had drawn me to the piece in the first place was not lost.

Aditya has an eye for detail that many people find quite challenging to deal with. Our carpenters definitely did. Working under his supervision, they soon realised that they could not bluff their way through this one! His friend and longstanding professional acquaintance, Amit Rajpal, the CEO of Marshall Wace, describes Aditya aptly as a man who has a relentless desire to learn through details. Aditya was visiting Amit in his office in Hong Kong and he was taken in by the office décor. Now, there are many who have complimented Amit and his team about their beautiful interiors but none, he says, who have drilled down to the nub of the matter like Aditya did.

He can't help it. Aditya believes that he must know every detail before launching into a venture, not because he wants to do everything single-handed, but because he does not want to be taken for a ride. He likes to be in control of the situation to be prepared for any eventuality. He is also able to focus on the goal, no matter how cluttered the world around him gets. Some days, when we were all at home, watching the news or discussing something completely unrelated to his work, I would see his eyes light up. An idea had struck him about a problem, maybe, which someone raised at work or perhaps he had hit upon a way to make more money for the bank—whatever it may have been, Aditya followed it through and was able to make sense through the noise that could be quite deafening at times.

To come back to the log of wood that was being prepared for a new life; exposure to the harsh saline water and sun for who knows how many years, turned it completely white. The designers tried quite a few things to bring colour back to the trunk, until

Aditya remembered that when they were children, their cricket bat used to be white and linseed oil would make it shine. Gallons of linseed oil were put into the trunk until it got back its original colour. Like I said, he pays attention to every detail and better still, remembers it all.

Today, the driftwood graces our living room. It is a part of our table, our sofa set and footstools. And like most of the pieces of furniture, art and artefacts that we have in our home, it has a story all of its own.

Aditya has always been completely involved with the home and his family. He is very house proud and is passionate about creating a good life for us all. That is why he is completely hands-on when it comes to picking up new furniture, thinking about how to create the best experiences for all of us and doing up the house.

In fact, the two of us have furnished our homes from scratch, picking up each piece and decorating each room and corner carefully to keep it simple and homely—just the way we like it. And nothing can stop Aditya from overseeing everything that happens in our homes.

When our flat in Prabhadevi (central Mumbai) in Vinayak Angan was being built, the lift hadn't been installed yet, but that didn't stop Aditya. He would climb up the stairs with the architect, explaining every detail and also making sure that his instructions were executed correctly. I was unable to be as active as I would have liked to be at the time because I had just been diagnosed with arthritis, but thanks to Aditya I didn't have to do much.

Aditya's involvement does not end with just the building of the house. And there are days when our friends who come visiting remark, “It is looking very different today. You seem to have changed everything and brought in new things.” All of that is his doing!

“Where there is love, there is life.”

M K Gandhi

22

STARRY SKIES AND WATERFALLS

WE SAT AROUND THE TABLE ONE NIPPY EVENING, UNDER A SKY full of stars. There was a lot of food, drink and laughter flowing freely when one of our friends asked Aditya, "How did you ever find this slice of heaven so close to the city?" We were at Rabasa (short for *Rab da asara*, which means under the merciful gaze of God or his *chhatra chhaya* as they say in Punjabi), a home that Aditya and I have built in Lonavala.

"All thanks to her," he said pointing towards me, "it is because she had so many conditions for the perfect home that I had to set the bar so high." As usual, he was having a good laugh at my expense but, therein lies a story. Or, should I say many stories?

Yes, I had many conditions as he says, for a home. Having been used to the open spaces and green surroundings in Ooty during my school years, I missed the outdoors. And so did he—the big gardens and large houses that he had grown up in were a far cry from the apartments that we have in Mumbai. I was also very keen to have a place in the open where we could enjoy a quiet moment by ourselves or have a raucous evening with friends.

However, maintaining and looking after a home with large open spaces can be a challenge, as many of you would know. So, I had a few things I knew that the house must and must not have. More important than my list, or should I say, more relevant to our story is the lengths he went to find the perfect house.

It took him over 10 years to find the perfect place. And having found it, he made sure that all things were in order. His enthusiasm in the entire project was infectious. He refused to hire an architect and Aditya and the builder would visit the site together, every week, to oversee the workers and make sure that things were being done just as he wanted them to be. His view is that if we were to live in the house then it must be a home that we love and have designed according to our tastes and needs, not an outsider's. I completely agree with him, which is why I had many conditions when we first thought about building a home there.

One of the conditions that I had was that we must be able to sit in the open without the problem of mosquitoes. All the years growing up, my parents would often drive us down to Lonavala (of course, at the time the drive was quite a long one but it was still an easy getaway from Mumbai) and I remember that come evening, there would be a swarm of mosquitoes that would make life miserable for us.

So, I had told him, I wanted a mosquito-free home. Aditya kept that in mind and before we finalised the deal, every weekend he would take off, with the architect, and sit out in the open through the evening and sometimes late into the night. Some nights, they sat up from 12 am to 2 am! What was the point, you ask? Well, that is how one can fully understand how a concrete structure can be built without obstructing the natural flow of air around the property.

Usually what happens is that the compound walls of the houses block the flow of breeze. Sitting in the dark, without fresh breeze, you are sitting bait for mosquitoes. Having found that out, Aditya raised the level of the house by about 40 feet and we have managed to keep the house mosquito-free even though we have three water bodies in the house. This was another one of my conditions, because I knew just how scarce and precious a natural resource it is in this area. He also made sure that there is ample sunlight throughout the day, which means that we do not have to depend on artificial lighting during the day.

Our property came with an old well that had fallen into misuse. We cleaned it and filled it up. Thanks to that, we are in position to not just have enough water for ourselves but also provide for the rest of the town if the need arises. Plus, there is a lake adjoining the property and an aqueduct that is used to carry water for the electric station nearby. We also have a waterfall, which is a story that beats Aditya's perseverance in building a mosquito-free zone around our property.

When we began building Rabasa, Aditya and I were both keen to have a waterfall on the property. Our travels had spoilt us. And we thought it might be fun to try and replicate the experience of being surrounded by the sound of water. Our architect checked out the property and said, "*Haan*(yes), it is possible, and it will cost around Rs 15–20 lakhs." It could go up too, if certain materials were not easily available.

"No way am I spending so much," Aditya said. But that did not mean that he wasn't going to get a waterfall. He buried his head into research—the internet, friends, experts, you name it. And he finally had a plan.

He called for a truck of large stones from Dholpur, a small town in Rajasthan that is known for its variety of red stones. The supplier cut them to a specified size and sent it to Rabasa. He charged us Rs 15,000, which was the most expensive investment that we made in the waterfall.

Since the height of the house had been raised, we had a natural incline within the property and he installed what is called a Tullu pump and a pipe to take the water up from the well and drop it from a height. The pipe was covered up with soil and voila, we had a home-made waterfall at a fraction of the cost!

However, it was not enough to build a waterfall, it had to sound right too. And with that thought in mind, Aditya launched us onto a waterfall tour—I don't know how many places we went to, just to study the way the stones were placed on the side of the hill and to record the sound the water made, as it splashed down. Every monsoon, for several years, we would get into our car and drive around from waterfall to waterfall, record the sound and if possible, bring a few stones back for our own contraption back home. And finally, he managed to get the sound right. Today, when anyone compliments him about the peaceful and beautiful space that he has created, guess what is the first story he shares with them?

“With mirth and laughter let old wrinkles come
And let my liver rather heat with wine
Than my heart cool with mortifying groans.”

William Shakespeare
The Merchant of Venice

23

A GHOST IN THE GARDEN

THE CARETAKER AT OUR HOME IN LONAVALA CAME UP TO Aditya in a state of panic, "You know the well that is there in our garden, ghosts live there," he mumbled.

"Ghosts, huh," Aditya asked him. "What do they look like?"

The caretaker, wiping the sweat off his brow, said, "They wear white. There are three of them—all women. They come and hold me by my throat as if they are going to strangle me."

Aditya didn't say anything else, except that he would look into the matter. Come evening, he called the fellow and said, "Put a charpoy for me out there, next to the well and a mosquito net. I am going to sleep there tonight and catch that ghost for you."

Taken aback, the caretaker tried to talk Aditya out of this adventure. Too dangerous, he told him, these were female ghosts who didn't stop at anything! "*Main hi maroonga na* (I will be the one they kill)," Aditya said, adding that he should organise his bed without any further ado. "*Kabhi aatey hain, kabhi nahin* (But they don't come every night)," he said. To that Aditya said he would sleep out every night until he had caught those ghosts.

The cold, the flies, the light...every hurdle that the man placed his way, he deftly climbed over. That was the last we ever heard of ghosts or spirits, or any complaint from our caretaker.

There is some history behind this that I have to let you in on. Our caretaker, who had been living on the property for several years, had been fermenting trouble at home. We had received many complaints about him raising a drunken ruckus at night, from some of our neighbours, apart from some other nasty stories. Aditya and I decided that it was time to confront him and find a replacement, and this man had got wind of it. He didn't want to give up his room on the property, and he thought that even if he did lose his job, the fear of ghosts would force us to abandon that patch of land and leave him in peace.

Clearly, he had no idea who he was dealing with. Not only does Aditya not believe in these things, he had also been told by the local priests that the land the property stood on was sacred. Especially, the well; a 150-year-old structure, the locals still believe that a devi lives there. Aditya was absolutely sure that this guy was pulling a fast one over us—ghosts were just a nice cover story.

The story of our Lonavala home, from the way Aditya built it to the way he maintains it and gets involved with every detail reflects his way of working in the bank. Colleagues and friends say that he knows how to aggressively defend his turf and is always ready to call out other people's bluff. His direct and blunt manner of dealing with things has helped resolve some tough conflicts, interestingly, one of which happened in the backdrop of our home in Lonavala.

He had invited a group of 30-odd people from HDFC Bank

to Rabasa. Aditya had been told that there was a problem in the team and there were two factions that had formed and neither was talking to the other. Sometime in the evening, Aditya asked the heads of the warring teams to walk with him and our three dogs, Scooby, Pogo and Bushka. It was quite hilarious. Neither had any idea how to leash and hold a dog, and while Aditya was there with them, he didn't offer any help or advice. They were forced to talk to each other and by the end of the walk, everyone was talking to everyone else. That night, the party went on till the early hours of the morning.

Rabasa is a place we get away to, from time to time and it has become a huge source for some funny stories. But it is also a place where both of us love spending our time, just by ourselves and with our friends and extended family. Aditya also constantly redesigns and repurposes spaces within the house. His creativity is best seen in our garden which constantly evolves as he creates a new corner for herbs or planting new fruit trees and flower beds. One time, he grew salad vegetables and then some years later, he turned that into a rose garden. Never afraid to experiment—he has tried his hand at everything—growing avocados, mulberries, alphonso mangoes, guavas! Every week, he checks in on the garden with our caretaker and then excitedly reports back to me and our friends on the fruits of his labour.

Aditya loves his garden, where he proudly shows off his green thumb. Of all his experiments, if I had to pick his favourite it would be the rose garden. The roses are his pride. We have a number of varieties growing in our garden. Aditya experimented with different planting techniques before he got what he wanted.

Many friends admire his handiwork and ask him where he

got such big, fragrant roses from. Aditya's replies instantly, "They have travelled from London to Lonavala, via Chandigarh." The thing is that the original rose bushes in his home in Chandigarh, which he replanted in Lonavala, were brought from London by a relative. Of course, over the years, the roses have taken their own shape, size and smell and are quite distinct from their European counterparts—but when Aditya puts it this way, it does feel good to know that there is a spot in the garden that has travelled from a faraway land.

> "Life is really simple, but we insist on making it complicated."
>
> Confucius

24

A SLICE OF HISTORY

AS ADITYA GOT BUSIER AND BUSIER WITH THE BANK, HE also had to spend a lot of time travelling. On most occasions, I travelled with him. On many of our travels, we have had some truly unforgettable experiences. One was with a sculptor from Odisha.

Aditya was being conferred an honorary doctorate by the Kalinga Institute of Information Technology (KIIT) University. The people who were hosting us were keen that we see the city and also appreciate its unique craftsmanship. They showed us some exquisite sculptures that really caught our eye, but when we wanted to buy one for ourselves and went around looking for a suitable piece at the local workshops, we were disappointed with what was available. Everything seemed mass-produced. Not like the ones we had seen.

We spoke to a few craftspeople and they told us, "Madam, there is one person who has a workshop in Puri who does not make copies. He makes just one of every sculpture, but he is very difficult to get." He truly was special and I could not take my eyes off the things that he had made out of stone. Every piece of sculpture spoke with a distinct voice. Aditya liked everything we saw and we ordered around a dozen-odd sculptures from him. As we were leaving, he said that he was really grateful for our attention and our admiration for his work and that he would like to gift us a unique piece that he still had to finish. We were intrigued, and wanted to know what he was making, but he would not say anything more about it. When we persisted, he relented and said, it is a Nandi (the bull of Shiva). That was it. He would not tell us the size or the stone being used, nothing.

Months went by and we got a call from him that the truck was being loaded and it would be making its way to our place. We decided to direct the truck full of sculptures to Lonavala, with a short stop in Mumbai, where some of the pieces had to be offloaded. The logistics in place, Aditya and I went and parked ourselves in Rabasa, with a few friends.

It was a Sunday afternoon; I remember it vividly even today. An elderly man wearing a dhoti was at the gate and he was asking for Aditya because he wanted to bring a truck into the house. Aditya went to check and to his utter surprise found the sculptor who we had last met in his workshop in Odisha, standing there with a huge grin playing on his face.

In his broken Hindi, Odiya and English, he told Aditya, "I wanted to see the future home for my sculptures," breathlessly adding that he had jumped on to the truck as it was leaving his workshop without any spare clothes or money on him.

Having come all this way, however, he was extremely embarrassed to show us the gift. All the other sculptures were offloaded but he kept saying that I don't know whether you will like it or not and he was hemming and hawing. Finally, we told him, we have kept a special place for our special gift and if you don't show it to us, how are we going to even figure out how it will look, etc.

When we saw it, we almost fell back in shock. It was massive! The Nandi towered over everything else and there was no way anyone could lift it out of the truck. I don't know how he had put it in, but we had to call a crane lifter to get the sculpture out and bring it into the garden. Now, Aditya had marked out a spot for it. I wasn't so happy with the chosen corner and was instead keen on a shady patch of green that had a clear view from the house. As the Nandi made its way into our home, I think it had made up its mind where it wanted to be. Because just as the lifters hauled it over the spot that I had had my eye on, the holders cracked and the Nandi landed with a thud, but without a scratch on it, let me add.

The sculptor was so happy with the house, the way his sculptures were placed and that the Nandi had chosen its perfect setting that he danced with joy. Seeing him so thrilled, it made us feel good too because after all, he was the creator of all these marvellous sculptures. He left soon thereafter, having livened up our afternoon and enriched our home with his sculptures made with so much love and care.

For the two of us, the story behind the things we own has always been more important than the brand or the price attached to it. Just as we had found these sculptures in Odisha, Aditya and I had run into some extremely beautiful and exquisitely crafted sculptures in Marble Rocks, an hour away from Jabalpur in Madhya Pradesh. He bought several pieces and the sculptor was so thrilled with his interest that he let us into the backroom to show us some of the work that was not for sale too.

However, there is one story that I have to put down here of our tryst with history (unknowingly) through old wooden furniture. A friend of ours who had migrated to the US called us up one day. He got talking about his mother who was living all by herself in Mumbai, ever since his father passed away a few years ago. His father was a famous writer and he had built himself a beautiful home in Khandala, which is where his parents had lived most of their lives. Once her husband passed away, however, his mother had packed up and returned to Mumbai. "She is emotionally very fragile and can't bear to go there anymore," our friend said.

He wanted us to help him sell the house. Aditya protested saying he was not the right person for this and he would put him in touch with the right people. But his friend was not one to listen. He wanted a trusted person to handle the sale and he told Aditya, "You have a lot of contacts. You can make it happen." We asked around and, in a few months, after taking several people to see the property, we found a very senior professional from one of the old Mumbai industrial houses who was very interested in the house. Once they confirmed, we called up Aunty A (let us call her thus) and put the two in touch, keeping our fingers crossed that since we had kept our commitment to our friend, this was the end of our involvement. No such luck. "The sale will happen only through you," Aunty A declared to Aditya, over a cup of tea one day. She added, "I have sold the house but I haven't sold the furniture. I want you to have it." We suggested that Aunty A bring it back to her place in Mumbai but she didn't want to do that. We could not say no.

So, the next weekend, Aditya and I went back and checked out all the furniture. We called her and said that we would load them all up and send it over to her. At that point, Aunty A said, "Go to the basement and see, there is more furniture there."

The basement was a disaster zone. Flooded, with a mass of wooden cupboards, chest of drawers, tables, sofas and beds floating in the water, it was a stale stinking mess. This was not all. Aunty A then declared that she wanted us to have the furniture that was in the basement as a token of her appreciation for our help. Despite our loud protests, she refused to back down from her offer. Aditya decided to take it back to the Lonavala home. He got hold of some really good furniture restorers who came and took a look at the furniture and told us that we were sitting on a pot of gold. *Yes, all right*, I thought to myself. It may be gold, but how are we going to make it shine again and where will we keep it?

A few months later, the carpenters and polish masters having finished their work, called us over. When we took a look at what was set out in front of us, I couldn't believe my eyes. It was truly gold and each piece shone like a unique work of art. Aditya called up Aunty A and thanked her profusely for the rather generous gift. And it was then that she dropped this bombshell on us, in the most nonchalant way possible, "It had to be good furniture. It belonged to an eminent personality who left the country."

"You see," she went on, "when this person had to leave India, he came to our house and told my father that he should go over to his place first thing the next day, and take whatever he could lay his hands on. Her father did as he was told and sent the furniture to Khandala. It is now a part of our homes in Mumbai and Lonavala. A blessing, or a gift from the gods—call it what you will, but it was an experience that I will never be able to forget.

> "Nothing happens without a reason (*Heturatra bhavishyati*)."
>
> Sanskrit saying

25

EVERYBODY KNOWS MR. PURI

DURING THE EARLY DAYS AT HDFC BANK, ADITYA HAD SCORES of people coming to see him in office every day. Some dropped in for a cup of coffee, some wanted a special deal and some just came to see just what Citibank's blue-eyed boy was up to.

Aditya's cabin door was open all the time, especially when he had friends dropping in, just for some chai and a quick hello. So, his colleagues always knew who was with him, when one of them was not in the room. There was this one gentleman, an old friend with connections to our family and friends back in Chandigarh, who would come by often. Aditya was cordial, enjoyed his time with the gentleman and that was that—when he came home, on some days, he would remember to tell me about his visitor, saying "Smiley, you know so-and-so had come again today." And we would chat about him and his old connections and leave it at that.

One day, one of Aditya's colleagues who looked after corporate banking at the time, came up to him and said, "You know, boss, I have signed off on the loan for your friend." Aditya looked at him completely unaware of what he was saying. "You know the guy. He was here just yesterday in your room," his colleague said.

Aditya looked at him straight in the eye and said, "I have no friends when it comes to the bank. If you have given him a loan, you better find a way of recovering it. If not, I will debit your salary because I don't know how you have assessed this."

That is how it has been with him and HDFC Bank. He has never used 'connections' to get things done, nor has he become a 'connection' that people can use for favours. He had sent out a message to all the HDFC Bank staff that when people claimed to know Mr. Puri, they had every right to turn back and tell them, "I also know Mr. Puri."

As the bank expanded and spread its branches all over the country, whenever anyone reached out to him for a favour, all he did was show them the rulebook and put them in touch with the relevant department head. "Once you break a small rule in banking, it opens the door for large-scale scams and that is the end of the bank. Every small gesture matters," he would say.

Friendship and banking are two different things. And this is not just with people who want something from the bank, but also for those who work with him. He keeps the two apart.

Aditya has quite a temper. Ask anyone and they will have at least a few stories of how they learnt the hard way that the boss's smile hides a sharp tongue. But no one can accuse him of being vindictive.

I would often ask him how he managed to have so many people who admired and adored him in the bank even though he was such a tough taskmaster. One day, a team member told me that even if Aditya lost his temper and was very demanding when it came to their work, he was very fair and made sure that everyone benefited from the bank's progress. His colleagues knew that he was not malicious, never bore grudges or harboured any ulterior motives. But the most important thing about him is that if anyone had a problem he would always come to his or her aid. His concern for them, no matter how serious or minor the issue, is what endeared him to his colleagues.

Once Aditya and I had travelled to Meghalaya for one of the bank's official reviews. During such trips, we would all gather on the final evening of our stay, for a large party. At most of these parties, Aditya and I would end up on the dance floor, jiving away to old Bollywood favourites and soon, almost the entire team would join us. These evening get-togethers would be a family affair. Some would come with their spouses and others would also bring their children—there would always be a crowd, no matter where we were.

One such evening in Shillong, as the party picked up pace, there was a lot of noise and chatter all around and someone (I don't remember who) decided that it was time to get to know each other better. People were asked to take centre-stage, introduce themselves briefly and speak a few lines about something they felt strongly about. A young man stood up, fished out his visiting card from the wallet and held it up, "This has given me more respect than anything else," he said. He came from a low-income family and growing up, he had faced a lot of discrimination. He continued, "In people's homes, they used to leave us standing at the door. Now the sofa is dusted down before we sit. We would rarely get wedding invitations. Now everyone calls us over. It is all because of this card."

"Thank you, Mr. Puri," the boy said, as he handed the mike

over to the next person. Aditya was very moved. He walked up to him and shaking the young boy's hand said, "It will be wrong if I let you believe that it is only HDFC Bank that has given you respect. You have built the brand and earned the respect."

Yes, it was true that HDFC Bank had opened the doors for young hopefuls like the boy in Meghalaya. But more important than giving them a job was providing them a place of work that was fair and just in its dealings with employees and people. When our people see fairness and openness at the senior management level, they become the best brand ambassadors for the bank, Aditya would say.

Over time, employees realised that the bank valued them, not just for their work but for being a part of the organisation. They eventually started to call the bank their own. This became increasingly the case as Aditya and his team launched many initiatives such as a welfare fund that takes care of the medical expenses of all employees and their families and tied up with many NGOs to help artisans and communities from the hinterland across the country.

He tells me that he made a conscious decision to keep things open and transparent all the time. "We shared all our options and salaries widely so that employees at all levels do well. I wanted them to educate their children, build homes and look at HDFC Bank as an employer with a heart."

I was lucky that I got to know the people at the bank at such close quarters. Thanks to Aditya and all the parties that he took me to, I became a part of the family. We would joke and sing and dance together and everyone knew that no matter how furious the boss had been in the morning, come evening, he would be more than happy to shake a leg on the dance floor.

I was always willing to join him for a dance and at one party, I heard the wife of one of the employees whisper as we walked past, "*Dekho Puri saab kaise vyavahar karte hain* (See how Mr. Puri behaves with his wife)." Our mutual respect and friendship, I believe, helped him create an environment of trust and good faith in the workplace.

> "Management is nothing but motivating other people."
>
> Lee Iacocca

26

SAYING IT LIKE IT IS

IT WAS A FEW MONTHS AFTER 9/11. THE HORRIFIC ATTACK ON America was still fresh on everybody's mind. Aditya and a small group were travelling to USA for a work trip. Amit Rajpal, who was the CEO (Asia) of Marshall Wace at the time, was with him and he tells this story.

"It was an investor's meeting and the who's who of global investing were there in the room that day. Aditya was presenting the HDFC story to the international community when someone in the room asked, 'What are the implications for HDFC post 9/11?' Now we all know how self-centred most American businesses are and for the likes of us, who have to deal with many such people in the course of our business, we have learnt to live with it. Not Aditya. Without so much as a pause, he called out the US-centricity of the question and then went on to say that HDFC Bank categorises countries into three. Category 1 is where the bank is happy to do business, category 2 is where the country is on the wait-and-watch list and category 3 is where the country is marked as a high-risk destination and the bank stays clear of all investments. The US, he added, is a category 3 country."

Aditya does not hesitate to speak his mind. Be it at home, with friends or associates, he is always blunt. For instance, there was this time that a very well-known industrialist asked for some favours. Not only was this gentleman very aggressive, but he also knew how to force his way through. He would argue loudly, always come with a large retinue of security personnel and refuse to take no for an answer. It took some blunt speak and some deft manoeuvring by Aditya to get out of that situation. But he did manage to do that, much to the relief of his colleagues.

Aditya believes that he was able to speak the truth to the powerful because he never compromised on his principles. He was able to say no to unreasonable requests from powerful and influential people because he never made any unreasonable requests himself. He says, "That is the truth—ultimately it is all up to the individual to set the boundaries in a relationship." Because he was so clear that he wasn't going to take any favours from anyone, he managed to have a good relationship with everyone.

He can build a rapport very easily, with people from all walks of life and even those he meets for the first time. I had once travelled with him to Bhuj, where the bank has been actively working with local artists and artist groups to create a more stable source of funds for the community. The artists had organised a *mela* at the hotel where we were staying and between Aditya and me, we managed to get all the guests to come and take a look at the goods on offer. Aditya spoke to the buyers, introduced them to the products and helped make quite a lot of sales that day. He gets to the core of the issue which endears him to people. That is what he does—he gets so invested in the project that he does not let go of any detail. It helps people trust him and the bank. The artisans at Bhuj adore him. Many years later, when a CNBC crew went to interview them about the bank and one of the interviewers said something about how the bank was charging them a high interest rate, one of the women said, "Please *hamare saab ke bare mein kuch mat bolo*(Don't say anything about him.)"

> "The most important persuasion tool you have in your entire arsenal is integrity."
>
> Zig Ziglar

27

THE MAHARAJA AND I

DURING ONE OF OUR TRIPS TO JODHPUR IN RAJASTHAN, WE were told that there was an auction of old furniture at one of the grand palaces in the city. Rajasthan is known for the grand and opulent lifestyle of its maharajas and the auctions threw up some really valuable pieces of antique furniture.

Once we reached there, I realised that we could barely afford anything. The furniture and other things on display were exorbitantly priced, but I was happy to indulge in some 'window shopping'.

Aditya's eyes suddenly lit up at the sight of a portrait. It was a large painting of a king dressed up in all his regalia. It had caught his attention from across the room and he walked up to the auctioneer, who, probably sensing Aditya's enthusiasm, quoted a huge price. There was no way we could buy that.

"What are you charging for? The portrait or the frame," Aditya quizzed. Taken aback, the man said in a louder-than-usual tone, "The picture."

"Ah," Aditya replied, "*Chalo, bach gaye* (Thank heavens). I want the frame only. How much will that be?"

The auctioneer was completely baffled. "Frame only?" He asked several times, until he finally quoted an amount that was a fraction of the price that he had asked for earlier. Aditya immediately agreed, and the intricately carved wooden frame was handed over to us. According to Aditya, he had had his eye on the frame right from the start—not the painting—but then, how would the auctioneer know that?

The frame, polished and shining, now hangs in our home in Mumbai. It holds a mirror and is a perfect prop for one of Aditya's jokes. When friends come over, after a few drinks go down the hatch, Aditya turns to them and says, "Let me introduce you to the great maharaja." He takes them by the hand and shows them the mirror. "There," he says, "that is king of all he surveys." When they turn to him flummoxed, he tells them the story. "The frame once held a king's portrait and it now has you."

Aditya never wastes a chance for a good laugh—be it at home with our friends or, (very often) at my expense or, in a room full of strangers. Some years ago, Aditya's work with HDFC Bank was getting recognised and he would constantly be invited for some talk or the other. He would turn many down but there was one invitation that both of us knew we had to honour. His alma mater, the Panjab University, wanted him to address their outgoing class of graduates.

Aditya was only too happy to do that and the two of us landed up in Chandigarh for the event. We were taken aback by the welcome that we received! There were posters lining the streets that had his photograph plastered all over and banners strung all along the roads, with the caption, 'Return of the prodigal!'

You know what Punjabi hospitality is like and needless to say, we were treated to a really good time. All the things Aditya wanted to eat, more importantly, all the things he wanted me to taste, were provided. We only had to mention the word and it was presented at our doorstep. The hour of his lecture soon arrived and the auditorium was packed—not a single empty seat in the room. He spoke at length about his journey in the banking profession, the ups and downs that had come his way and how hard work and passion have been his constant companions in every venture. It is always interesting for me to be a part of these events, because when he looks back on the life that we have led, I am often surprised by the things he is able to bring up. There have been times, I had no idea about what he had been going through either.

Coming back to the auditorium, it was time to take questions. A student turned to him and asked, "You spent many years here. Tell us, which were your favourite haunts." He paused for a moment and then with a sheepish grin said, "See, whatever I am about to say does not take away from what I have just told you. All that still holds. Hard work, passion, *sab jaroori hai* (everything is necessary). But the truth is, while I was here, I worked the hardest at eating *bun anda* opposite the English department. My friends and I timed our visits such that we were there just as the English classes got done. I am sure you all know why we did that," he said (as I am sure you do too, dear reader). The room burst into laughter.

> "The measure of a man is what
> he does with power."
>
> Plato

28

EVERYMAN'S BANKER

IN THE JANUARY OF 2019, WE TRAVELLED TO KUTCH. WE HAD planned this for a while and I am glad we were able to go and see the spectacular Rann of Kutch before the pandemic of 2020 forced us indoors. On our way back home, we stayed over.

As I said earlier, whenever we go to a new place, Aditya makes a list of the best food spots in the city and then makes sure that we cross each one off the list before we leave. Bhuj has a famous *doodhwala* cum *mithaiwala* (milk and sweetmeats seller) whose fame has spread well beyond the city. He sits outside his home, a tiny room with a veranda, which doubles up as his store and attends to the queues that snake through the lanes and bylanes of the area. People from neighbouring towns and tourists passing through Bhuj make a beeline for his shop, so much so that he opens at 7 a.m. every day and runs out of stock before noon.

The most sought-after item on his menu is thickened milk served in clay pots. During our stay there, we had to taste this delicacy. Truth be told, I wasn't looking forward to this because milk is something that I avoid at all times. But Aditya would always be ready to taste something new. It was decided that he would head for the *doodhwala* while Amrita and I would go around the market and do our own thing.

We were in the midst of shopping for some beautiful, colourful jewellery when Aditya's voice boomed over my phone. "You have to come here, *now*." We quickly made our way to the most crowded corner in the market where I could see Aditya excitedly waving through the sea of people around him.

He had just tried a glass of the famous thickened, sweetened milk and he wanted me to taste it. I scrunched up my nose, not only because I am not a fan of the stuff but also, because we had had a really heavy breakfast. I gulped it down and believe it or not, I asked for another! Never have I tasted such delicious milk and Aditya had a good laugh at my expense that morning.

Many of Aditya's colleagues were also with us that morning. As we got ready to leave and I think we were headed out of Bhuj later that day, Aditya excused himself for a moment and disappeared. He was back shortly, beaming from ear to ear.

He had been chatting up the *doodhwala* about his daily earnings, etc., and discovered that he made a neat pile of cash every morning. Aditya asked the man, "Ever considered keeping an HDFC swipe machine and banking with us?" An astute businessman, he negotiated and struck a good deal for himself.

There have been so many times that Aditya has done this that I have lost count. We have travelled all over the country and everywhere we went, there was always a gleam in his eye when he spotted an opportunity to expand the HDFC Bank footprint into non-metros and small towns.

He has been passionate about the bank since the very

beginning. I have never known a time when we didn't think or talk about it. Also, I have always been so involved with his work, in terms of listening to him and discussing any problem that may be bothering him that it feels as if I have been a part of his professional life as much as being his life partner.

I have felt the pain of losing loyal and talented colleagues and I have also shared his joy when the bank kept winning awards and accolades while never losing sight of his quarterly earnings. What have I learnt from him, people ask me nowadays. Having watched him so closely, is there a lesson or two that I can take away.

I find it impossible to look at things this way. Of course, there is a lot to learn about him and from him, but it is a continuous process. However, there is one quality that I admire in him and I wish I had the same—his ability to observe things carefully and find simple solutions to complicated issues.

One of his oldest colleagues and friend, Abhay Aima, once recounted a story about how Aditya knows him even better than he does himself. "In my 58 years, I haven't met someone as street-smart as him," Abhay said. That, in addition to his ability to gauge people and deal with everyone according to their preferences, he believes, separates Aditya from others of his kind. Abhay had at one point in his long career with HDFC Bank contemplated leaving. He had been offered another job that he was quite keen to take up. He went up to Aditya for a chat. This was quite common; his colleagues have always freely discussed job offers, new entrepreneurial opportunities and other such issues with him that one would hesitate to talk to a boss about.

Aditya heard him out and at the end of the conversation, Abhay recalls, he came up with an insight into Abhay's behaviour and asked him to think about that before coming to a decision. The very next day, Abhay turned down the offer. Their friendship is such that they both expect and command complete loyalty from each other without ever having to say anything to that effect.

Aditya understands people and his friends and will always do his best for them. But, if he does not see eye to eye with someone, he can be quite blunt and that can lead to a feeling of hostility. For example, there was a very senior colleague who was looking to change jobs but he was also trying to see if he could negotiate a better deal within the bank. He came up to Aditya and said that he had an exciting offer and that they were pushing him to join immediately, but since the bank had a long notice period, there was a bit of an issue and so on. Aditya said that he need not wait for the notice period to get over. He could leave after finishing the coffee.

This attitude of his does lead to some negativity towards him, but he always has just one reply, "I do what's good for the bank." This was the motto that he held close to himself even in his early Citibank days—be it dealing with unhappy employees or manipulative vendors and customers. The trick to running the bank without fear or favour is to always do what is good for the bank, not for oneself or one's friends or a specific cause. That's his secret.

> "True knowledge is not attained by thinking.
> It is what you are. It is what you become."
>
> Sri Aurobindo

Home is where the heart lies

04

29

THE JEWEL IN THE DESERT

TRAVEL HAS BEEN AN INTEGRAL PART OF OUR LIFE TOGETHER. I have been with Aditya on umpteen trips, all over the world. And like I have said so many times, thanks to him, I have tasted the most exotic food and seen the most amazing sights that there are to be seen.

However, there was one place that Aditya seemed to be in no hurry to take me to although I was very keen to go there. The city on my wish list was Jaisalmer, about which I had heard a lot from my family and friends. It seemed like a magical and charming place with a lot of things to shop for. But every time I suggested Jaisalmer, Aditya ended up planning another trip.

His reluctance to go there, I later learnt, was that there was no direct flight to Jaisalmer and it was a long drive from Jodhpur, nearly eight hours. So, he would invariably not have the time because he didn't really enjoy long car drives.

My repeated requests finally bore fruit. For our twenty-fifth wedding anniversary, Aditya decided to fulfil my wish. He planned a long trip to Rajasthan with Jaisalmer on our itinerary.

We took off for 10 days, driving around Jodhpur, Jaisalmer and Bikaner. There were other stops in between too, and quite often we would stay in beautiful havelis and palaces in the small towns around these cities.

On the day of our anniversary, we happened to be at just such a place called Gajner. It is on the outskirts of Bikaner. The Gajner Palace is a beautifully maintained resort. It was built by Maharaja Ganga Singh as a hunting resort and is believed to have been the favourite of several viceroys and maharajas in its time. Located at the edge of a forest, it has a lake within its premises and is surrounded by lush green open spaces all around.

On the day of the anniversary, we had a quiet lunch. There was a table that had been set up in the forest reserve across the lake, under the bright winter sky and I remember that the weather was perfect. The sun felt good on our backs, taking the edge off the winter chill that gets quite severe in this part of the country.

From where we sat, I had a view of the resort, which was where most of the rooms were and also where we were staying. What's going on? I asked Aditya, because I could see a flurry of activity. As far as I could figure out, there weren't too many guests at the hotel. It was us and a few families, so few that we barely met each other even during meal times.

Aditya was equally baffled. "*Kuch ho raha hoga* (something must be up)," he mumbled. Come evening, I realised how good a conman he is, or maybe, you could say, just how gullible I am to fall for his tricks every time! Having pretended to not know anything about all the bustle and activity at the hotel, it turned out that he was the organiser-in-chief.

In the evening, as we were finishing our walk around the garden, he said, "*Chalo*, let us walk to the edge of the property." We slowly went up the path that ended in a forest. The forest loomed dark in front of us and the light was quickly fading from the skies. It was winter and it was also getting a bit chilly.

We turned to go back to the resort, but I stood transfixed—the resort rose in front of us like a sheet of gold. Aditya had organised for the entire place to be fitted out with tiny lights and he had also organised the evening walk route in such a way that the lights would dazzle me in the way that they did. When you looked at it, coming out of the darkness as we did that evening, it looked like the most amazing place in the world. That was not all, however. The evening had just begun, so to say, because he had arranged for a band of local musicians to play and the food was specially catered for us too. I had got what I most liked—a surprise, my favourite Rajasthani music and food in a five-star setting in the middle of the forest. But wait, there is more to our anniversary trip, there is more drama and lots of surprises in the story that I will tell you next.

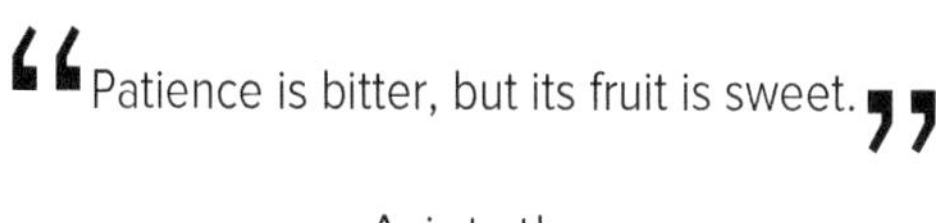

Patience is bitter, but its fruit is sweet.

Aristotle

30

KARNI MATA AND HER MESSENGER RATS

OUR TWENTY-FIFTH ANNIVERSARY TRIP WAS MEMORABLE FOR more reasons than one, yielding a lifetime of memories. But the moments we spent in a unique temple in Bikaner are unparalleled.

When we were planning the trip, suggestions and recommendations had poured in from all quarters. Our friends and family had come up with lists of places to see, temples to visit, forts to photograph, the food to eat and a lot more. One thing everyone had agreed was that our trip to Rajasthan would be incomplete if we did not visit the temple of Karni Mata.

The temple is located about 30 kilometers from Bikaner in a place called Deshnok. It is famous for its rats that move about freely in the temple. There is no floor space visible in that temple and visitors are advised to wear socks or some sort of foot covers when they walk around. Let me add here that this is not because the floor is dirty. The entire temple premises are spotless and there has never been any case of illness or rat-borne diseases in the area. The visitors are advised to cover their feet just so that they do not feel uncomfortable, which is only to be expected as we are not used to having rats running over our feet.

We wore shower caps on our feet. We have friends in the area who knew me well enough and they said, "Please wear a covering otherwise you will run out of the temple. Also, please do not scream when you see so many rats. They are harmless"

As per the last count, there were close to 25,000 rats in the temple. No one kills a rat and if one dies a natural death, there is always another one that takes its place. Even more interesting is the fact that the place has never had any major disease outbreak, neither is there any foul smell, nor is the area dirty.

Among the black rats of the temple there are three white mice, which are believed to be the sons of the goddess. The local lore has it that the maharajas of the region would visit the temple before a battle and would not leave until they spotted at least one white mouse. They are a sign of good luck and the goddess's blessing. Even today, visitors to the temple are believed to have the Mata's blessing if they see a white mouse.

Our friends had warned us not to get our hopes up too much because the white mice are quite difficult to spot. There is a joke that in the days of the past, when kings came looking for a white mouse, the priests spent the entire night finding one and then held it up for a royal inspection. The king would go home happy that the goddess had blessed him. They told Aditya that if you can spot one white mouse, consider yourself lucky, seeing three is believed to be a miracle.

We reached the temple early in the day, maybe the day before we went to Gajner Palace. Our son Amit's friend had accompanied us and he said he would shoot a video of the temple and our puja. As we stood at the entrance and the camera swept over the floor and slowly moved up towards the idol, we could not believe what we were seeing.

Three white mice lined up in a row sitting on the parapet of the temple, staring at us! We were absolutely thrilled and everyone, the priests included, kept telling us that there was no greater blessing that was possible. The Mata loves you, they said.

We stepped into the temple, I was walking very carefully, although everyone told me that I should not be scared. The rats were used to humans walking around them all the time and had learnt how to deal with their fears! But I am terrified of rats and I was taking no chances. I had been forewarned that I should not scream at the pandit when he was performing the aarti. That was another point of stress and I wanted to be extra careful to avoid any sudden movements.

A special aarti had been organised for us and we all went up to the idol and waited for the pandit to complete all the rituals. The words of our friends kept running in my head, "Please don't scream, please don't scream at the idol." However, the best-laid plans of men are dismantled by the gods. And within minutes of the aarti starting, I let out a loud scream right at the pandit because a rat had begun climbing up my leg, having found a way in through the salwar! You tell me, would you not have done the same?

> “Faith is the bird that feels the light
> and sings when the dawn is still dark.”
>
> Rabindranath Tagore

31

WISH LISTS

ALL THOSE YEARS AGO, ADITYA INSISTED AND, GOT HIS WAY, with a small wedding. I went along with him but then, *meri bhi kuch armanein thi* (I had some desires too). I kept telling him that because of him, I couldn't do so many things that as a young girl, I would have loved to do. He would laugh and say, "I will make up for it."

I was not the only one who felt let down with his diktat, let me add. Did I tell you that his father, who had wanted a big wedding too, went back to Delhi and organised a grand reception without us! Aditya owed me a grand celebration and on our thirtieth wedding anniversary, I decided that it was high time that I did something about it.

I decided to have a big celebration with all the ceremonies and rituals that go into a big fat Punjabi wedding. My only regret was that I no longer fit into all the beautiful lehengas and cholis that I would have easily slipped into, way back in 1978. But never mind, the joy of dressing up and having all our friends and family celebrate with us made up for all that. We had a big sangeet ceremony at a friend's home. A choreographer was appointed and we all had a few dances assigned to us—for Aditya and me, it was an old favourite, '*Udein jab jab zulfein teri*' (a song from the old Bollywood hit *Naya Daur*) that we danced to.

We went through the sangeet ceremony, mehendi, wedding reception and all the rituals. Aditya was a good sport, he didn't object to anything and made sure that our guests had the time of their life. We had a large gathering for our reception where our friends—new and old—were treated to the choicest cuisines from around the world. Of course, there was unlimited laughter and happiness on the menu.

A marriage is only as strong as the two people in it. Our strength comes not just from standing by each other in the good and bad times, but also from our willingness to indulge each other. It was my desire to relive my wedding moments, with all the pomp and splendour that was missing the first time around. But without Aditya's support and his wholehearted participation, I would never have been able to do that.

Another desire I had, being the Bollywood film fan that I am, was to experience an iconic scene from the movie *Aradhana*. The movie, directed by Shakti Samanta, is an all-time favourite. I can watch it as many times as anyone plays it for me. The scene that I had played over and over in my head was a song shot on the Himalayan Princess ('*Mere sapnon ki rani*') that had Rajesh Khanna and Sharmila Tagore. I wanted to go on that train.

Even today, this song is considered as one of the most romantic songs shot on a train. It has a very interesting story behind it too. The song had to be shot at two locations: one was on a film set on Mumbai where Sharmila Tagore was filmed, sitting in a replica of the Darjeeling Express, while sneaking glances outside and these shots were interspersed with Rajesh Khanna driving down the scenic route that the train takes from Bagdogra to Darjeeling.

Aditya knew about my wish and he organised a trip for the two of us with Amrita a couple of years back. We took the train to Darjeeling and played the song while we travelled along the route. It was a lot of fun and an experience that I will never forget.

A hands-on family man, Aditya does his best to make every wish come true. With me and the children, Amit, Amrita and Bhaswati (our *bahurani*, Amit's wife) and most of all, our grandson Rian, he goes out of his way to make sure that no desire is unmet. At our Lonavala home, he has created a bouquet of experiences for us—a corner inspired by Europe's al fresco cafes, a fireplace for warm family conversations, swimming pools and waterfalls that create a soothing atmosphere that helps us all relax and have a good time.

He entertains us all with good music, great food and a table full of laughter. He plays his all-time favourite songs and singers—his tastes range from Harry Belafonte and the Beatles to Sufi music, ghazals and the golden era of Bollywood music when the trio of Mohammed Rafi, Lata Mangeshkar and Kishore Kumar ruled supreme.

Once we had all travelled to Banaras and Aditya and me had just been treated to a spectacular performance of the Ganga Aarti, which is a synchronised ritualistic dance with lit brass lamps to worship the river Ganga. It is performed by male priests who dance with lamps, conches, flowers and other such paraphernalia and is a sublime spiritual experience. Amrita had come along with us, but at the time of the aarti, she happened to be elsewhere.

Although she rushed back to make it in time, she missed the show by seconds. She was crestfallen, but I consoled her saying that she could watch it the next time we were in the city.

Aditya isn't one to give up quite so easily. Without telling us, he went up to the priest and pleaded for another round of the aarti, even if it was done on a smaller scale. The priests were reluctant but I don't know how, Aditya managed to convince them, to Amrita's great joy!

> "In your light I learn how to love.
> In your beauty, how to make poems."
>
> Jalal-Ad-din Rumi

32

TENNIS FANS AND SWIMMING POOLS

GREECE HAS A SPECIAL PLACE IN OUR LIVES. ADITYA'S EARLY days with Citibank led us to Athens and we have travelled around the country, several times since. On one of our trips, Aditya decided that he would take back an olive sapling for our home in Lonavala. The olive tree is commonly found in the country and he had bought a sapling that came covered in a thick layer of soil (to keep it fresh and safe on a long journey).

He looked at me, his eyes gleaming, and said, "It will grow very nicely in the Lonavala weather and we can have olives from our own garden, think about it, Smiley." When he has that look in his eyes, I know that nothing I say will make him change his mind. And after all these years, I have become so used to him that I always carry an empty suitcase, bubble wrap and mask tape wherever we go. You never know what we get from where! On that trip, an olive plant came back with us which is now growing beautifully in our garden.

The olive tree is just one of the experiments that Aditya has conducted in the garden. He loves working with the soil, seeds and is constantly trying out new ways to grow roses, vegetables and herbs. On most weekends, that is where you will find him—in the sun, caked in mud but extremely happy.

He has a green thumb and also likes showing off his plants to all his friends, regaling them with stories about how he nurtured them to life or the pains he had to go through to keep them breathing as he carted them across the ocean. The result is that our garden has a unique character and anyone who visits Rabasa cannot help but be enchanted by it and the stories it holds.

It is not just the garden; the entire home is a patchwork of memories. Every corner tells a story. But first, let me take you to the swimming pool in our Lonavala home. It holds a special place and has a special story as it is closely linked to our grandson, Rian.

Rian was very young at the time. His parents, Amit and Bhaswati, were working in Singapore then, and we used to visit them very often. On one such trip, as were leaving to come back home, Aditya told Rian, who was expected to spend the coming winter in India with us, "See you soon, we are going to have some good times in the pool when you come."

Rian was quiet and when Aditya prodded him a bit he said, "Dadu, you only have a paddle pool and it is cold. I don't want to swim in the cold water." *Bas*, Punjabi *ko thes lagi* (it hurt his Punjabi pride). Aditya kept saying, "I have to do something about the pool. How can he say it is a paddle pool?" Back in Mumbai, he was on the phone with our decorator and he spent hours googling swimming pools and heating facilities—it became like a mission he had to undertake.

"My grandson has challenged me and I have to prove to him that my pool can beat the best in the game," he said. It took six months for Aditya to rebuild the pool. Under his supervision, the old pool was taken apart and a new one, significantly larger, was built to a whole new set of specifications. It came with temperature controls and we even had a plastic woven blanket cover, custom-made for the pool, just so that the pool could be covered every evening and the water stayed warm for an early morning swim.

The new pool took a lot of effort and went through several iterations. But that is the thing with Aditya—he has what we call *junoon* (passion). Once he is challenged, he will never give up unless it is truly an impossible task. When Rian came home that winter, he was thrilled to see what his *dadu* had done for him and till date, the two tease each other about their swimming pool challenge.

Rian is also a tennis fan and Aditya has looked for every opportunity to take him to some of the best games in the world. I remember, one year, it was the French Open and Rafael Nadal was playing against Dominic Thiem. Aditya took us all to watch the game and Rian was thrilled. We had a very close view of the court and Rian was so excited that he could barely contain himself every time his hero, Nadal, scored a point. Amrita was with us too and she supported Thiem and the two of them kept encouraging their players, shouting over each other's voices, in the breaks. And then finally, at a very crucial moment in the match, when the players were evenly poised and the game was, maybe, tilting just a little bit towards Thiem, Rian kept jumping up and down on his seat until he could take it no more and shouted, "Come on, Nadal! I know you can do it!" Everyone burst into laughter and Nadal shot him a bemused glance before wiping himself down with the towel and heading back to his corner. For Aditya, nothing beats the thrill of giving his family what they want, to the best of his abilities. Be it me, Amrita, Amit and Bhaswati and of course, Rian, no wish is too small or too big for him.

> “Good business leaders create a vision, articulate the vision, passionately own the vision, and relentlessly drive it to completion.”
>
> Jack Welch

33

WHERE THERE IS A WILL...

THE PASSION WITH WHICH ADITYA TAKES UP A TASK IS admirable; I am always in awe of the way he keeps his focus and does not give up, but even more impressive is the way he gets into the details of the work. When he was retiring, some of our friends had written about their experiences with him (you can read them at the end of this book) and everyone had the same thing to say. He gets into the details and gets things done.

Oof, I don't have the patience that he has. I would much rather look at things and wish for them to happen, instead of making them happen. Not Aditya. He is the one who pursues every wish till its end. Sometimes, I curse myself for pointing things out to him because I know that he will not rest till he gets it done.

Some years ago, for instance, we had gone to Masai Mara. It was a lovely family trip. Amit, Bhaswati, Rian and Amrita were there too. The place we stayed at had a beautiful fireplace. Charming, warm and very welcoming—we found ourselves gathering around it every evening. One day, sitting by the fire and enjoying a drink and chatting away, I said, it would be nice to have a corner like this at home too.

I regretted the words the moment they came out of my mouth, because he instantly had that gleam in his eye. He insisted that I take photographs of the place, capturing every detail. Within days of our return, Aditya and our architect set off for Lonavala, the pictures stored on their phones. They spent days figuring out the best spot for the fireplace. However, we were very sure that we didn't want to want to break any part of the house to build one and that was proving to be a hurdle. The architect and his team kept telling us that it would be quite impossible to create a cosy corner without breaking something down.

I would have given up at that point and said, *chalo*, we can live with what we have. Not Aditya. He kept going back and surveying the house until he finally found a spot on the terrace that would work on all counts and also met with the safety standards—now we have built a fireplace and a neat little dine-out with tables, chairs and a bar. He went through books, YouTube tutorials and spoke to numerous people and in the end, he managed to get it built.

I now think twice, before opening my mouth. He breathes and sleeps a project once he takes it up. This is also how he built our Goa home. I was not so keen on another house, because I feared the burden of maintenance. But once Aditya sets his heart on something, he never steps back. He knows how to get around my objections too, after all these years. He cajoled and coaxed and finally said that no decision would be taken until I gave the go-ahead, but that I should take a look at the plot.

It was not a large piece of land, but it stood right where the Mandovi river flows into the sea. The location was gorgeous, but I was still hesitant. Aditya wasn't giving up—he took out a piece of paper and he drew a rough sketch of the house he had in mind. "A boathouse made of glass, that's what you will have here," he told me. How can anyone resist such a beautiful description of a home? Could you have said no after that?

Having convinced me, Aditya reached out to our friend, architect and Goa resident, Edwin Menezes, to design the place for us. But he put a really stiff condition: the house had to be ready in six months, before Amit and his family came to India for their winter break. "I want to spend Christmas and New Year in our new home with my family," Aditya told Edwin.

This was an impossible target by any standard. Edwin was also hesitant to commit, but within a few weeks, he told us that it could be done. What made him change his mind? "You did," he told us. "The passion with which the two of you are working on the house, everything will fall in place," he said. Aditya's *junoon* can be infectious and let me warn you, if you are not careful, it can infect you too!

I immersed myself in the construction of the house. I sourced local stones, looked for easy-to-maintain furnishing material and affordable interior fittings and artefacts. This has been the way we decorate our homes—we keep it simple, stay away from soulless expensive materials and as much as possible, go with local materials.

For instance, our furniture in the house in Goa is made of rosewood. I discovered while talking to a shop owner in the village that this is the best wood for the local climate. I was buying a set of tables from him and we got chatting. He had just bought an entire truckload of furniture from an old Portuguese-style villa whose owners were relocating. I asked him what he would charge for it, quickly working out that this would save us a lot of time, given that we had so little of it. His eyes lit up at the thought and he gave me a really good deal, because I said he could send the truck directly to our home, saving him storage costs and other overheads. We had built such a rapport that as I was about to leave with the tables, he asked me to wait. "*Aap ke saath mujhe beimani nahin karna hai* (I don't want to cheat you)," he said. He took the tables to his workshop at the back of his shop and said he would have them delivered a day later, after replacing the fake stones with original tiles that he had stowed away for a quick buck later. His tables (with the original stones) and our furniture have added to the large quilt of memories that our homes are wrapped in.

Over the years, we have come to really love the Goa way of life and have made many friends. The local shopkeepers and restaurants also recognise us and it feels like home. Aditya has even had a drink named after him! A small local restaurant has it on its menu and it is called 'Mr. Puri's Italian delight'— feni, which is a local brew, mixed with Campari; the drink can give you quite a buzz, let me warn you.

Aditya's favourite drink is single malt whiskey and of course, rum. Actually, rum holds special memories for him as his father was in the air force. In their canteens, rum was cheap and always available. He loves spending time with us at home, with a drink, instead of going to a large party or a noisy pub. And in our home, the wine and whiskey flow as freely as the food and banter.

> “There are basically two types of people.
> People who accomplish things, and
> people who claim to have accomplished things.
> The first group is less crowded.”

Mark Twain

GLIMPSES INTO ADITYA'S JOURNEY

After looking for her for years, Aditya found Smiley in an arranged marriage set-up. At their roka (engagement) in 1977 in Delhi.

Bound in holy matrimony on 28 January 1978, at the Arya Samaj Mandir, Santacruz, in Mumbai.

Aditya with Amit and Amrita at their Shantiniketan Bungalow in Delhi during his Citibank days.

Aditya and Amit with the first car they bought in Saudi Arabia, a deep blue Audi.

Aditya and Smiley at their 30th wedding anniversary party at Madh Island.

Fulfilling Smiley's long-held wish to take the train journey, Aditya posing on the Himalayan Princess train in Darjeeling with Amrita and Smiley.

Aditya was thrilled at the birth of Rian, Amit's son. Seen here holding the baby with Amit and Smiley.

Aditya with grandson Rian, London 2022.

The Nandi which chose its own place to watch over all at Rabasa, Lonavla, their vacation home.

The heated pool that Aditya built for Rian at Rabasa.

The Puri family with Vijay Amritraj, at the French Open at Roland Garros, June 2019.

Planting a tree with Pujya Swami Chidanand Saraswati on a visit to Parmarth Ashram, Rishikesh.

The family on vacation in London, 2022.

Aditya displaying his sporting skills. He has passed on his love for football to his grandson, Rian.

FORGING LASTING BONDS AT WORK AND BEYOND

Aditya on a weekend excursion in Glyfada, Greece—the first international posting with Citibank.

Aditya travelled to different countries for work. With Citibank colleagues in New Zealand.

Aditya with Margaret Thatcher at their house in Kuala Lumpur when he headed Citibank, N.A. Malaysia, 1993. Behind them is Shaukat Aziz (Aditya's boss at the time, now former prime minister of Pakistan).

Mahathir bin Mohamad (left), former prime minister of Malaysia and Shaukat Aziz (centre) with Aditya (right).

Aditya escorting Manmohan Singh (then finance minister) with Deepak Parekh, at HDFC Bank's launch in Mumbai, 18 February 1995.

HDFC Bank's ADS listing on the New York Stock Exchange in July 2001.

Aditya guiding HDFC Bank to achieve new heights.

At the workplace, Aditya calmly resolves matters as he understands the situation from both sides.

Master banker Aditya at St. Regis Hotel, with Gary Mehigan of Masterchef Australia fame.

Ajay Banga (CEO of Mastercard Worldwide) standing behind Smiley at the French Open Stands at Roland Garros with the Puri family, June 2019.

Aditya giving a speech at the American Indian Foundation.

The many awards which Aditya received over the years. Illustration by Smiley Puri.

34

PUZZLES, FOOTBALL AND CHEAT SHEETS

RIAN IS ADITYA'S *JAAN*, THE APPLE OF HIS EYE AND JEWEL IN his life and everything precious that you can say. There is nothing that Aditya does without him in mind. The two are like old pals; *chaddi* buddies, Bhaswati (Rian's mom and Amit's wife), calls them.

When they are together, it is difficult for us to figure out who is the child in that relationship. It has always been like that—from the time he was just a toddler, Rian and his dadu were inseparable. Aditya would always look for ways to engage with him and knows how to become a child with him.

When Rian was about 5-6 years old, Amit was in Singapore at the time and we would visit often. Aditya would also drop in during his many travels, so we got to spend a lot of time with him. Aditya would always take a gift along and after some time, he decided to ask Bhaswati for suggestions for a good present for Rian. She said, "Papa get him board games."

Aditya must have searched for as many as he could find and on our next trip, there we were in their house with an armful of board games. Bhaswati had a good laugh at us, but she was even more amused when she saw that most of the games that Aditya had picked up were for older kids. "How am I to know, as if I looked at the age group the games are meant for," Aditya said in his defence.

The next morning, we saw Aditya and Rian sitting down with a game meant for children who were at least 3-4 years older than him. Aditya was patiently explaining it to him and also, when things seemed to get too complicated, he was simply ignoring the rules, to play it his way.

Soon, that became the practice. Aditya would land up with board games meant for all ages and he and Rian would spend hours figuring them out together, sometime completely changing the rules. "No right or wrong here," his dadu would tell him, "we keep learning and keep having fun."

Some of the games required advanced mathematical skills and we were surprised to see Rian pick up complex concepts quite quickly under Aditya. Not only did he grasp things easily, he was very interested in teaching us all that he had learnt too. On our trips to Singapore, I would find Rian waiting outside my room early in the morning with a blackboard and a box of chalk in hand. He would wait outside the door because his mother wouldn't let him come and disturb us, but the moment we emerged, he would not let us go. He became the teacher and we were his students.

Aditya would encourage him to speak his mind always. And when we were among friends or at a party, the two would sing and dance uninhibitedly. It doesn't matter if you can sing or whether you know the steps of a dance, just going up and doing it is what is important, Aditya told him.

Our relationship has grown over the years and all the time spent together, doing the things that we have, has helped us build a rapport. We have a good laugh about their antics even now, about the time that he and Aditya had struck a secret pact on sweets, for instance.

Rian wasn't allowed too many chocolates and every time we visited, Aditya would carry a huge bag full of chocolates, which Bhaswati would confiscate. One day, Rian came and complained to Aditya about how he never gets to taste them at all. The two then struck a deal that the sweets would be handed over to him directly, but he would have to exercise control and not have more than just a couple, every day.

Rian has also learnt many tricks from his dadu. He has had first-hand lessons on how to pull a fast one over the competition in a game of football. Ever since Rian was very young, from the time he could kick a ball around actually, Aditya and he would enjoy a game of football. As he grew up, he became better and faster and soon Aditya found it difficult to keep up with him. But Aditya is also very competitive and he wasn't going to let his grandson win so easily and so, he would trip him, when he saw him racing past once too often.

"Dadu, you can't do this." Rian would get all sweaty and angry. Unfazed, Aditya would reply, "See, you saw me with (Lionel) Messi, right? (There is a photograph with Aditya and the Argentine footballer that was clicked during one of the World Cup matches.) He told me I can do this."

Rian knew his dadu was not quite telling him the truth and

he would fume and fret and go running off to his dad. But soon he would be back again, for a game in the sun. The two share a special bond and I have to say that he too has not been spared the Aditya brand of humour.

He was a bit older when this incident occurred, by then he could understand that Aditya was quite well-known and that his photograph hit the newspapers quite regularly. Rian asked, "Dadu, how do I get rich and successful?" Aditya said, "One is that you have to work very hard, then you must learn how to get along with people and the third thing is that you have to know a lot of things and remember them. I will help you and as a prize I will buy you a convertible so that when you go to Harvard, you can take all the girls for a spin." Amit and Bhaswati roll their eyes at their father's sense of humour but Aditya never passes up a chance for a good laugh—not even with his grandson.

"A human life is a story told by God."

Hans Christian Anderson

35

NO FRILLS, NO FUSS, NO TIME FOR SUPERSTITIONS

AMRITA AND I ARE ADITYA'S WARDROBE MANAGERS. LET ME get this straight, we have had to take up this task. Not because he asked us to, but because he pays absolutely no attention to what he wears. And believe me, it can be embarrassing.

His favourite outfit is a T-shirt and a pair of shorts or an old pair of jeans. In the early days of our marriage, I never paid much attention, but gradually I began asking him to wear a different shirt, choose a different colour combination and so on. His standard response was and is even today, "I don't know what to wear. I pick the first shirt or T-shirt in the cupboard." I have given up and now I make sure that I put the shirt that I want him to wear right on top of the pile, whenever we have to meet friends or attend an important event.

I am reminded of his complete disinterest in clothes and brands whenever his friends and colleagues tell me that your husband is a man in a hurry. It is like he is always on a deadline, with little time for anyone or anything else. But does that make him an impatient man? Maybe not. Because he has ample patience to counter an argument (with me, especially) or find a solution to a problem—be it building a fireplace in Lonavala, a swimming pool for his grandson or as I am about to tell you, finding the right footrest for a Saraswati idol in our home in Mumbai.

During our trip to Puri, we had bought some really large idols of different gods and goddesses. Most of them are now in our homes in Lonavala and Goa. But there is a beautiful idol of Saraswati, the Hindu goddess of knowledge, which is here in Mumbai.

From the minute he set eyes on it, Aditya had picked out a corner for the idol in our Mumbai home. It is a stunning piece of work, but quite heavy. Aditya felt that we needed to create a base for the idol so that the weight would not crack the floor and to protect the idol against the daily wear and tear caused by sweeping and swabbing the floor. But how does one find anything sturdy enough to hold such an idol? Many people suggested making a stone slab and placing the idol on top of that, but that would have defeated the purpose.

We asked around, but nothing worked. He tried several different kinds of wooden bases, but every piece cracked under the weight of the idol. Finally, he had an idea. He went off to the local butcher in our area and asked him what he used as a base for all his cutting and chopping. They showed him this thick log of wood that bore marks of many knife cuts. Aditya then asked him if he could get him a similar log and split it into two. The fellow looked at him rather strangely, but he said, "No problem, *saab. Manga lete hain.* (No problem, sir. Will order it.)"

Aditya is religious, but he is practical and he has absolutely no time for superstitious and irrational behaviour. Many of us are not able to make that distinction. When we were getting an idol of Shiva for the house, Aditya had a taste of just how silly some of our beliefs can be and we got a glimpse of how he counters such advice.

We have a Shiva idol in our bedroom. It is huge and majestic and seems perfectly at home in its spot. However, when we brought it in, several people (friends and interior decorators and such other professionals) told us that it would bring us bad luck if we kept Shiva in the bedroom. Aditya was not convinced, but he didn't dismiss their ideas outright. He dug into the subject, speaking to many people and reading up about the worship of Shiva until he had no doubt that there was no basis to the fears being expressed by people.

He did his research thoroughly and found out that Shiva represents cosmic energy and is the destroyer of evil. He keeps the world in balance. He is omnipresent and his physical representation is man's effort at embodying all his properties for human worship.

He asked me if I was bothered by the fact that so many people seemed to think that we had made a mistake. I am like him, religious but not superstitious, and had no doubt in my mind that no god can ever be vindictive towards his devotees.

There is one thing however where Aditya lets his emotions trump over reason. His children. He worries endlessly about them—if Amit had a fever, Aditya would be up all night. When Amrita was younger and she was out late, he would be the one checking on her every hour. Even today, he cannot handle it when they fall ill. He can't even watch them taking an injection!

Everyone who knows Aditya will tell you that he is a hard-nosed astute banker. He has nerves of steel and during crises, his team at HDFC used to marvel at how calmly he weathered every storm. But all of this falls apart when it comes to his children. He is a bundle of nerves when it comes to Amit and Amrita.

However, he is also both mentor and friend to his children. When they have problems, he spends hours trying to find a way out and talking to them, to me and anyone else who matters, until things are back on track. He is always rational and hears them out even when they don't always agree on things.

Amit, for instance, had enrolled for his chartered accountancy, but decided to switch to a different line. Aditya questioned him thoroughly, helped him make up his mind and then start over, on a different path altogether. As for Amrita, it took him some time to come to terms with her choice of becoming an actor, but today he is her biggest fan and supporter. How did that transformation happen? Now, that is a story that I have to tell you.

> “A man is but a product of his thoughts,
> what he thinks, he becomes.”
>
> M K Gandhi

36

AN ACTRESS IN OUR HOME

FOR AS LONG AS I CAN REMEMBER AMRITA LOVED THE MOVIES. As a child, she liked to dress up and sing or dance in front of the mirror. I remember several big events at our homes in Kuala Lumpur when she was barely knee-high, but even at that age, she was always camera friendly and never too shy to pose for the photographers.

She tells me that the first time she fell in love with acting was when I had taken her to a play at Prithvi Theatre in Mumbai, which is one of the oldest performance theatres in the city. She was just 13 years old. Five years later, she went on stage herself with a professional theatre group and never gave up on her dream ever since.

However, when she first told Aditya about wanting to become an actor, he was aghast. It came as a shock to him. A Punjabi father, a banker that too–imagine his daughter wanting to be an actor! He laughs about that moment now, saying, "I am a Punjabi landowning family's son. My father served the country. And then my daughter said she wants to be an actress—I have never been more destabilised in my life."

Initially, he couldn't react at all. But after some amount of ignoring and hoping the problem would disappear, he began diverting her attention to other tempting career opportunities. From advertising to journalism, he tried every creative trick in the book to make her change her mind.

Amrita has a rather humorous account of how her father tried to take her mind off acting and how she finally managed to get her way. I am going to tell the rest of the story in her words.

> "After graduation I told dad that I wanted to do my MA in acting but he was absolutely against that. 'Of course, you should do your MA,' he said, 'but not in acting.' I needed to do something that offered a steady job. 'Journalism,' he said. I had a good hold on language and that's what I should do.
>
> 'Go to Colombia,' dad said. All right, that's what I thought I would do. And I was all set too. I had completed 16 years of my education in India, which was a prerequisite for going abroad at the time and I applied for my GRE exams. But guess what, I was confronted with the worst fear that I have since childhood. Maths!
>
> I know everyone finds it very interesting that I, the daughter of the ace banker, Aditya Puri, is afraid of numbers. But that is life! Dad finally accepted that he could not put me through the stress of dealing with maths, or maybe he could not deal with a stressful me. Never mind what the reason was, a degree in journalism from Colombia was taken off the table. Phew!

But he said, 'You know what, you will be a fabulous copywriter.' He has this amazing knack for convincing me that what he wanted me to do was actually my idea. I went along with that too. For a year I tried my hand at copywriting, which by the way, he thinks I am fabulous at. But then I realised that I spent all my time at work waiting to get out and get into an acting gig. What was I doing really?

I quit my job and decided to follow acting, full time. Convincing dad was the issue. But if he is anything, he is rational and knows passion when he sees it. And I never let up. I told him one day that if I don't see myself on the big screen, then after I die I would come back just to go on the big screen. My family says that I am a drama queen. Well, I guess I was just living up to my name.

I don't know what the turning point was, but I think we had spent two years arguing and perhaps everyone just grew tired of that. I am extremely close to my parents and it was difficult for us to see so much conflict at home. Besides, I understood what his fears were—acting is not an easy profession. It is unreliable and is full of disappointments. Now I tell people, do it only and only if there is nothing else that you want to do.

For me, there was nothing else that I want to do. Even as a child, I would sing and dance for my family all the time. I would try mom's sarees and lipstick and pretend I was Sridevi. I was obsessed with the song '*Mere haathon mein nau nau chudiyaan*' (a Bollywood hit from the movie *Chandni,* which starred Sridevi and Anil Kapoor) and performed it at all family weddings and wherever else the opportunity presented itself.

Dad perhaps thought I would give up once I saw just how difficult this was. But I didn't, and I think that helped him come around to my point of view.

The big break (for me) was when I got a call from my casting agent about auditioning for the movie *Aisha* (a hit romantic comedy starring Sonam Kapoor and Abhay Deol in lead roles that released in 2010). I went to Anil Kapoor's office after I was chosen. I was given the script and told which character I would play.

Frankly, I wasn't very excited about the role initially. I played this rather unsophisticated, wannabe girl. It was dad who told me to take it up without any further ado. 'Just do it,' he said, 'this is the opportunity of a lifetime.' After that, there was no looking back and he got completely involved with my work.

He would vet the producers and directors I was going to work with. It was really embarrassing. I remember during *Kai Po Che*, he insisted on coming along and meeting the director! Now he doesn't do that. He trusts me and also, he doesn't think like that anymore.

Today, my biggest fans are my parents. My dad watches every show I am in and even if he does not watch the entire episode, he makes sure he is glued to the parts that I am in. He reviews my work and diligently gives me feedback. He even calls up people and asks them to watch me on screen, much to my embarrassment."

Aditya, as Amrita says, is her biggest fan. He has lengthy discussions with me about how talented she is and how she played a part really well. Nothing matters to him except the happiness of the children—this is as true today as it was when they were younger. I remember a time when Amrita was in school and we had just shifted back to Mumbai. She was being bullied in school and Aditya would drop her off every morning, just to reassure her and make her feel confident to face up to whatever happened in school. He has been as much of a steady influence on Amit too. When he was changing jobs and when he wanted to set out on his own, Aditya was there for him every step of the way.

> "All power is within you;
> you can do anything and everything."
>
> Swami Vivekananda

37

TWO HEARTS BEAT IN ONE-PART I

THERE ARE SOME DAYS THAT ARE IMPRINTED ON YOUR MIND like it happened yesterday. For me that day is 10 February 2016. It is so clear that I remember the time on my watch and how my eyes fell on the minute hands—it was 6:55 a.m.

"I have a back pain, right in the centre," Aditya said. We all think we know what to do when we fall ill, having read so much about how to give first-aid or what one must and must not do in a crisis, especially now that we have everything at our fingertips. Well, I thought so too. But life teaches you better.

I looked at Aditya and thought that no one had said anything about a pain at the centre of the back being a cause for concern. And yet he looked really unwell, this didn't seem like one of those regular aches that can be dealt with. "Smiley, just rub some balm or spray on it and let me lie down," he said.

"No," I told him, "you are not lying down." Maybe it was the look on my face or the tone of my voice, or just the pain was getting so severe that he could not talk, Aditya didn't protest. He stood there quietly while I grabbed whatever I could lay my hands on—my credit card, loose change and anything else that seemed important to me at the time.

With the help of our staff at home, I guided him to the elevator and out of the building where we lived at the time. Amrita was asleep and Amit and Bhaswati were in Singapore. But that morning, I knew I had to do this myself. I don't know why but a voice inside was telling me to run, that there was no time and I had to move quickly.

Aditya was a bit surprised with the urgency with which I was moving. "It is just a back pain," he said. "call the doctors, there is no need to go to the hospital," he went on. But the voice in my head drowned everything else out. "Run," it said, "you have very little time at hand." I stuck to my plan. I will call the doctor but, let us first get to the hospital.

I ran out of the building, right into the middle of the road to hail a cab. There wasn't too much of a crowd as the city was still waking up, but you know how it is in Mumbai. The streets are never empty and I got quite a few strange looks from passers-by and the cars whizzing past me that morning. I wasn't going to drive because I was taking Aditya to the Hinduja Hospital where parking is a big problem. In any case, I was in no state to drive.

My street, which usually has plenty of the black-and-yellow taxis (this is well before the age of Uber) was empty that day. I was panicking with every passing moment when I finally saw a cab coming towards us. I jumped in front of it. There was an elderly man at the wheel who was just as surprised with my behaviour as Aditya was.

We made it to the hospital in record time. I don't know what I told the driver but it must have worked because he got me there as fast as anyone can in this city. We rushed into the emergency ward and I remember yelling, "HE IS HAVING A HEART ATTACK! SOMEBODY, ANYBODY, DO SOMETHING!" I just could not shake off the dread that had caught hold of me nor could I ignore the constant voice in my head that said that I was racing against time.

While we were in the cab, I had called up a few people we knew. Among them was our close friend, Dr. V Srinivas or Srini, as we knew him. He and his wife were among our closest friends and at the time, he was among the most senior doctors in the hospital. Thanks to him, things moved quickly and Aditya was rushed into the care of specialists. Once I got that out of the way, I called up the office and told them that Aditya was unwell and that we didn't want to tell anyone about it immediately. I don't know where I got the presence of mind or the strength to do all this; I can only thank God and my guru for coming to my aid at the right time!

My nightmare wasn't over yet. Aditya was inside the operation theatre and two doctors were waiting outside for me. One look at their faces and my blood ran cold. They seemed hesitant to talk. I took a deep breath and said, "*Jo bhi hai* (whatever it is), it doesn't matter. Just tell me."

Aditya had had a massive heart attack. This was not just an ordinary heart attack but he had a condition which in a layperson's vocabulary is called the 'widow-maker's clot'. If there is a scale of heart attacks, this is right at the top—it is the most dangerous there is. Doctors told me that it can happen suddenly when a key artery that moves blood to the heart gets almost or completely blocked. In the worst-case scenario, the clot rips an artery open and the person dies on the spot. It is a silent killer and few people survive the attack.

"It is only because you wasted no time at all that he has been able to make it this far," they said. My mind was still racing from all that they had told me. I knew that bringing him to the hospital on time was just the beginning of a long battle that lay ahead. "Lay it out for me," I told Srini. "What are the next steps?"

He said that we could do one thing that will give him a fair shot at life, but it would be a big risk. He explained that a team of doctors would work on him and help shatter the clot, gently, without bringing on another attack. The danger would be that sometimes, despite the best intentions and efforts of the medical team, such a procedure can induce another attack. Even after it was done, Srini added that Aditya would have to be kept under very close observation for at least two days for the doctors to know if the procedure had worked. There was just a 20 percent chance of survival and I told him that we should take it.

Until now, I was the only person in the family who knew the extent of the emergency. My son and daughter-in-law were unaware and Amrita only knew that we had gone to see the doctors.

About an hour-and-a-half later, the treatment that the doctors had put him on began showing results. He was still in the red zone, but I could see that there was hope returning to the doctors' faces. I called Amit, only to remember at that point that he was out on a holiday in a remote place that did not have a phone connection! Anyway, I spoke to the lady who worked with them and left a message that he should call back as soon as he got it.

The next call was to Amrita. I told her the full story in a calm voice. She is so close to Aditya that I knew she would be really upset. All this time as I sat in the hospital lobby, walked up and down the foyer, spoke to doctors and nurses—I was all alone. There was a source of energy that I never knew I had and I was calm.

As I paced up and down, a lady came up to me and said, "*Suna hai tumne apne husband ko bachaya hai* (we heard you saved your husband)." And soon there was no end to people coming up and holding my hand, sitting with me and the nurses and attendants smiling and saying what a brave thing I had done.

I was sure that God had carried out his will through me and while I can laugh about it all now, it was really scary for me at the time. It seemed like someone had pulled out all the life from me, in a flash. But there was no way I was giving up on his heart, while mine beat strongly—that much I know.

> "The Self is the one reality that always exists and it is by the light of the Self that all other things are seen."
>
> Ramana Maharshi

38

TWO HEARTS BEAT IN ONE-PART II

WITHIN ABOUT 48 HOURS OR SO, I GAINED THE CONFIDENCE to know that Aditya would beat the clot; I felt that he would fight back and regain his health. My family and friends gathered around quickly. Amit and Bhaswati came down as soon as they heard the news and Amrita was by my side throughout. Our first step was finding him the best doctor for a heart condition like his. There are many doctors in the city who have done commendable work on the heart, but this was a rare condition and not too many people had dealt with similar cases at that time in the country.

We knew that a bypass was needed. But we wanted Aditya to get the best care we could give him. Hence, we needed a doctor we could trust. A friend recommended that we consult Dr. S Bhattacharya.

Amit came along with me for the appointment while the rest of the family stood guard at Hinduja Hospital. I had heard from many people before how a single meeting can change one's life. That is how I felt when we walked out of Dr. Bhattacharya's chambers that day. He was calm and completely confident that he could bring Aditya out of danger. Over the next couple of months, we found that it was not just him but his entire team of assistant doctors who were just as cheerful and friendly. I credit them as much as anyone else for Aditya's recovery process.

While Dr. Bhattacharya reassured us about his availability and care, there was one hitch. He could not go to Hinduja and if Aditya were to have him as a doctor, it would have to be a hospital close to his home which turned out to be Breach Candy Hospital on Warden Road.

It took some amount of patience and a lot of perseverance on our part to get Aditya into Breach Candy Hospital. But I am glad that we finally did. Because it was not the hospital that mattered at the time, it was the doctor. Without Dr. Bhattacharya and his team at the hospital and in his chambers, Aditya would have had a much more difficult time. After the operation, the doctors congratulated us and told me that I should watch my step now—Aditya was going to come out of hospital a much younger man, now that he had a young heart in his body! I laughed and said that I had nothing to worry; he may have a younger heart but what about the rest of him? That was the same.

I remember those days like it happened yesterday. The last day, as Aditya was about to be discharged (this still brings a smile to my face), when one of the doctors who had been looking after him came up to him and asked, "Have you thanked the person who saved your life?" Aditya looked a bit puzzled because we had thanked everyone—from the doctors and nurses to the ward boys who had been such pillars of support through the entire ordeal. A twinkle in his eye, the doctor said, "Your wife. You owe your life to her."

> "Pleasure and pain are only aspects of the mind. Our essential nature is happiness."
>
> Ramana Maharshi

The last word

05

39

THE COMPLETE MAN

THERE ARE SO MANY FACETS TO ADITYA'S CHARACTER THAT it is difficult for me to put it all in one book. However, through the stories in this book, I have tried to bring out as much of the man that he is—the funny, interesting, foodie, energetic and always positive side of my fellow-traveller, companion and closest friend. He is:

Always positive: Nothing is impossible for him. I remember numerous instances when the situation at work seemed very difficult. People would tell him how there was no solution to a problem. He always kept the faith, be it a professional or a family crisis. And his standard phrase is that there is no magic wand, but there is light at the end of the tunnel.

Bold and sensible: It may seem like two very different qualities. How, you may ask, can a man be both? He is not afraid to take big risks, be it in the form of big projects with the bank, his career or our plans for the future. But at the same time, he is not a risk-taker. He does enough research before taking a big step. He keeps things simple, is grounded and down to earth at work and at home.

Careful and wary: Aditya's rule is never to give a loan to someone who cannot pay it back. He has stuck to this all his life and once he does give a loan, he works hard to ensure that they keep their commitments to the bank. This attitude has helped him and the bank perform well, consistently, year after year. In our personal lives too, he pays attention to our investments and does not fall for rash promises.

Unassuming and humble: Aditya has never put on airs or made a lot of noise about his achievements. And whenever people congratulated him about the great heights that HDFC Bank had achieved, he had just two things to say: one is that this is not my work alone, it is because of the team. And secondly, '*hum to naukar hai bank ke* (I merely serve the bank along with my colleagues).'

Team player: All through his work life, Aditya always believed that the bank was able to achieve the great heights that it did because they had a good team. He respected his teammates and has always given credit where it is due. This has earned him the lifelong loyalty of those who have worked with him. At many places that we have travelled together, people would come up to him with stories about how he had changed their life and he would always say that this is not his doing alone, but that together they have built the HDFC Bank brand and that is why they have all benefited. I would always ask him how so many people loved him so much even when he was known to be blunt, someone who never hesitated to tell people when they were wrong. The reason is quite simple; it is because Aditya is a fair person. He does not bear grudges and, he makes sure that everyone gets credit for a job well done. There have been several instances where people have come up to us to thank him for ensuring that they got due credit, in terms of money and accolades for a job well done.

Always generous: Aditya's parents and grandparents instilled a lot of values and principles in him. They taught him to respect everyone and be humble but there are so many other things too that I can't list all of them here. They told him, you must never put your hand out with your palm facing upwards, like you are asking for something. Always put your palm facing down, as if you are giving away something. He believes in this and is extremely generous, to this day.

A passionate banker: He is a man with infinite passion. Ask his colleagues and friends and everyone will tell you that he is so deeply committed to his vision of the bank that nothing could keep him away from his work. Even when he was about to retire, during the lockdown, he was living, eating and breathing the bank. That is what makes him different.

Loving, family man: I think this is very evident in the stories here. Because Aditya worries so much about all of us—me and the children—I have had very little to worry about. When Amrita is out late, he is the one who stays up till she is home. When

Amit has a problem, Aditya is the first one he turns to. The most relaxing thing for him is to spend an evening at home, sharing stories and listening to music. His favourite song, the one we danced to for our thirtieth wedding anniversary, is '*Uden jab jab zulfein teri, kunwariyon ka dil machle*' (With every flick of your hair, you force the hearts of all young men to miss a beat). It never fails to make him smile.

Incurable romantic: He is an extremely romantic husband, leaves no opportunity to surprise me and is very sensitive to my desires. The two of us share a love for music and one song that Aditya sings for me is an old ghazal that was sung by Pankaj Udhas,

> *Chandi jaisa rang hai tera*
> *Sone jaise bal*
> *Ek tu hi hai dhanwaan gori*
> *Baaki sab kangaal*
> (You look as if you are covered in silver and your hair is all gold, true wealth is yours alone, the rest are all broke.)

There are others who know him best as a boss, mentor, friend, innovator and visionary industry leader. You can discover Aditya through their words. Only when we get to know all these aspects, do we get a complete picture of the man, don't you think?

I am really overwhelmed and grateful to all those who responded so eagerly, making time despite their packed schedules to tell us their thoughts and understanding of Aditya. To them belong the last words in this book.

“कर्मण्येवाधिकारस्ते मा फलेषु कदाचन।
मा कर्मफलहेतुर्भूर्मा ते सङ्गोऽस्त्वकर्मणि॥ 47॥

(You have a right to perform your prescribed duties, but you are not entitled to the fruits of your actions. Never consider yourself to be the cause of the results of your activities, nor be attached to inaction.)”

Bhagavad Gita, Chapter 2, Verse 47

40

THE MAN WE KNOW

A world class banker and entrepreneur

When I first met Aditya, I knew he was a world-class banker. My first impression, however, was that in addition to being a banker he is an entrepreneur and a down-to-earth individual with a deep connect to Indian culture, values and the people of India. What I saw was not just a traditional banker but also an entrepreneurial business owner. *Bharat ki mitti se juda hua banda hai* (son of the soil) is what I thought to myself. I have been deeply impressed with his ability to manage relationships, big and small, with ease. In my multiple meetings with him, I have always got some new ideas from our conversations, which have helped me in growing Reliance.

I know that Aditya loves watching cricket and playing golf and it is likely that he will have more time for all that, now that he is a retired man. But I am also sure that his fertile mind coupled with a passion for business and economy will not keep him away from businesses and building the Indian economy and coming up with more path-breaking ideas.

(*Mukesh Ambani, chairman, Reliance Industries Ltd*)

Nurturing and protective, a role model

What Aditya has achieved with HDFC Bank is nothing short of the exercise and display of genius. He has created an institution that is the pride of India. But honestly speaking, when I think of him and his success, I first think of Aditya as a terrific father. I know that he has been nurturing and protective, yet great company and very affectionate all at the same time. All of us at this stage in our lives when we look back, I think, we are going to be prouder about what we have achieved as parents than what we have achieved in our careers. And I think Aditya is a role model for us. I wish him great luck in his future endeavours and as we say in Punjab, I send him a massive jhappi and good wishes.

(*Anand Mahindra, chairman, Mahindra Group*)

Gutsy and methodical

Rarely does one come across a colossal figure such as Aditya Puri who has shaped the industry in such a dramatic manner. I have had the opportunity of meeting him and talking to him a number of times and there has never been an occasion when I have left the meeting without being struck by how entrepreneurial and forward-looking a man he is.

It is very rare to find people in professional life who can manage both risk and bring to the table entrepreneurial energy at the same time. It is a rare combination and I think HDFC Bank has been very fortunate to have a gutsy, but equally very methodical, process-oriented leader like him at the helm for over 25 years.

(*Sunil Mittal, founder and chairperson, Mittal Group*)

Patient listener and good lender

Aditya Puri has built up from scratch, an institution that broke all dogmas and barriers. He joins the league of people who have played a pivotal role in their nation's march towards developing and building the country as an economic super power. To quote J P Morgan and his unforgettable maxim, "You cannot pick cherries with your back to the tree," Aditya has been the perfect picker, he has picked good people, good ideas, good clients, good ventures, good practices and good processes. And over the years, over many enjoyable discussions that we have had over our urban–rural divide, with me trying to urge [him] to lend more to rural India, I have enjoyed and cherished all those moments over the many cups of coffee that we have had. [He] has been a perfect patient listener and a good lender because when he lends his ears he lends it fully. His journey runs parallel to India's post liberalisation rise into a super power and as I reflect upon what is the core reason behind this great success, the one that comes to mind is trust. He has won the trust of his clients and if I may venture to say so, trust is a better complement, a bigger compliment than even being loved.

(*Mallika Srinivasan, CMD, Tractors and Farm Equipment Ltd*)

Aspirational, confident and straightforward

Aditya is a role model for any bright young star aspiring to be a great CEO in any sector of the economy, anywhere in the world. He is aspirational, confident, straightforward, value-based, grounded in reality and a result-oriented leader. He walks the talk and the results are there for all of us to see. The achievements of HDFC Bank under his leadership are legendary—the largest bank by assets, largest bank by market capitalisation, the most innovative bank, the safest bank for investment, the private bank with the least NPA, the bank with the best brand; the list goes on and on. When I think of Aditya, I am reminded of the adage, 'Miracles we do in a jiffy; the impossible, we take a little bit of time.'

(*Narayan Murthy, founder and chairman emeritus, Infosys*)

Mentor, institution builder and a warm human being

What Aditya has built (with HDFC Bank) is awesome. It makes everyone of us proud—proud as Indians, proud as professionals that something like this institution has been created by Aditya.

He is a great professional and I have always benefited from his inputs and advice. I will continue to look to him for guidance, for his mentoring (capabilities) and inputs in making the Indian financial sector even better.

I would also like to talk about our personal relationship. I have had the joy of visiting Aditya at home and he has always displayed a certain sense of personal warmth, which (my wife) Pallavi and I have both noticed. We genuinely believe in the niceness of Aditya, but for us Smiley is also special and we deeply care about this relationship.

(*Uday Kotak, founder and CMD, Kotak Mahindra Bank*)

A genuine entrepreneur

I first met Aditya over 25 years ago when he returned to India after giving up a comfortable job with Citibank to [create] a banking start-up with HDFC. At that time, I was running the Infosys banking software division called Finnacle. I was not able to convince Aditya to use the Finnacle software, nevertheless, we became good friends.

To me he is a genuine entrepreneur. When he came back, the bank was just an idea, a license. It had the pedigree of HDFC and of course, it had the capital. At that time in 1994–95, India had not had a new private bank for more than two decades since nationalisation. So, it was really starting from scratch with a piece of paper and designing a bank. And it's astonishing what Aditya has done in 25 years, to take this start-up from a gleam in an eye to the third largest company in India by market capitalisation. He has built the entire system, the risk management, the credit and everything else that makes banks work.

(Nandan Nilekani, co-founder and non-executive chairman, Infosys and former chairman, Unique Identification Authority of India (UIDAI))

Makes the impossible possible

Aditya is a lesson in leadership. I can epitomise his qualities in three broad thoughts. He makes the impossible possible. He is not in the limelight but is in the limelight. And his work-life ethic. Aditya has done what was seen as impossible, when you looked at it say 15 years back. Twenty-five years ago, it was probably a dream, to get an Indian bank into global reckoning as it were. And Aditya did that wonderfully well with HDFC Bank. The second aspect is his being off the limelight and being in the limelight. I think this has profound meaning and importance—by that I mean Aditya himself never sought the limelight, that is very clear to everybody around him. He never basked in the limelight. However, his achievements spoke for themselves and caught the limelight. The third aspect is his work–life ethic. I have not seen this at close quarters, but one used to always hear that he was a stickler for his personal timing, his personal space. I think that is a great space to be in where you work to your ethics and that ethic brings in automatically the balance in your life.

(K V Kamath, former chairman, ICICI Bank)

Unrelenting clarity, unparalleled focus

There are many extraordinary things about Aditya, but I will share a couple of thoughts here. First is his unrelenting focus on clarity. In business, this has enabled him to build simple business models with unparalleled focus on education. Many times, he is able to cut through things that others may feel are complex obstacles. The second thing I want to talk about is his focus on customers. Be it the customers in the rural area, the farmers, or shopkeepers, Aditya goes to great lengths to understand their needs and then, carefully constructs a value proposition that benefits them. I am completely taken by the simplicity with which he can come out with this value proposition. Aditya cares deeply for India and believes in what India can achieve and has great aspiration.

(*N Chandrasekaran, chairman, Tata Sons*)

Never lets an opportunity go by

Aditya Puri has, in many ways, revolutionised Indian banking and has proved that you can build a world class financial institution from scratch in the country. When India grows and aspires to become a large economy, a middle-income country, we would be having at least half a dozen, if not more banks in the top 100 financial institutions in the world. And all the banks who would aspire to get in this list would look and say that we were inspired by Aditya Puri and he paved the way for us to reach that scale.

I first got to know him when I came to India to be at the helm of Hindustan Unilever. He came to us with a team to find out how we could deepen the relationship between the two organisations and in his typical style, he asked me whether I had banked with HDFC. In those days I used to bank with multinational banks, having been away from India for so many years. Today, the maximum amount of my dealings, in a personal capacity, I do with HDFC Bank. So that's Aditya Puri for you, a quintessential banker who never lets an opportunity go by. A proud Indian and a great nationalist, he has got many years of service to the nation ahead of him.

(*Sanjiv Mehta, CMD, Hindustan Unilever*)

FAMILY TREE

Rai Bahadur Brij Lal Puri & Bebe
Shambhu Lal & Lal Devi Puri
Kaushalya & Wing Commander Tapishwar Puri
Aditya and Anita (Smiley) Puri
Amrita Puri
Amit and Bhaswati Puri
Rian Puri

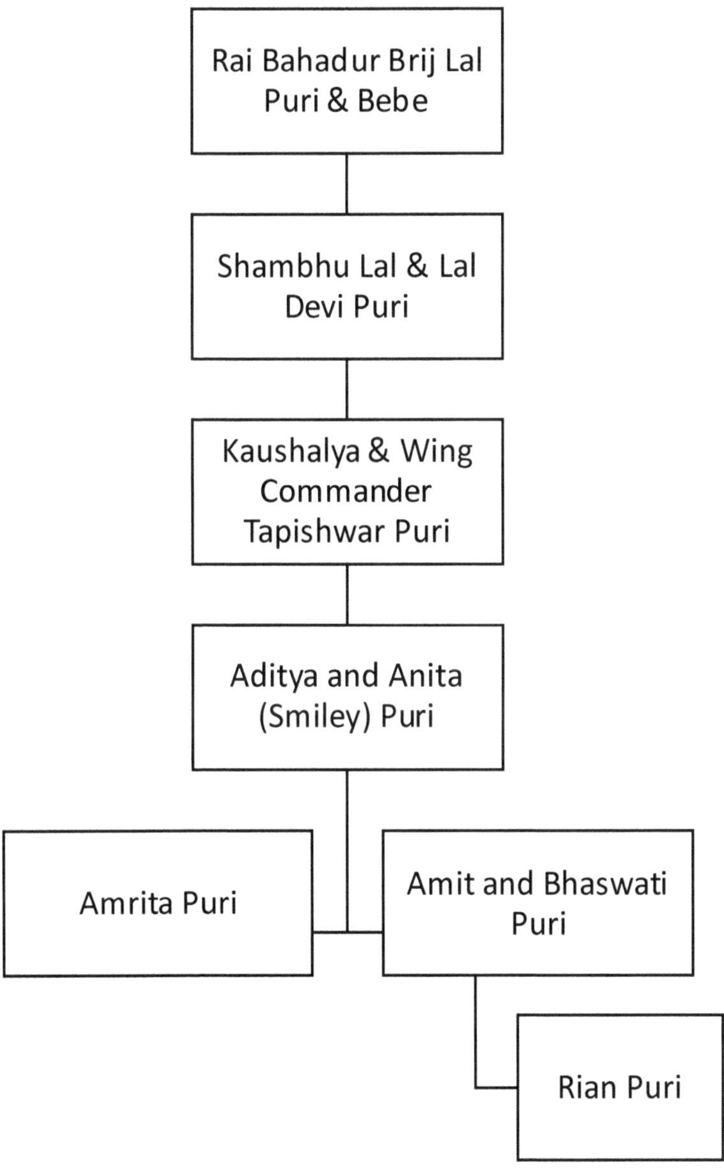

"All the world's a stage, and all the men and women merely players: they have their exits and their entrances; and one man in his time plays many parts, his acts being seven ages"

As You Like It, William Shakespeare

CONCLUSION

ADITYA HAS SMOOTHLY MOVED ON TO THE NEXT CHAPTER OF his life and I am so happy to see him passionately pursue his dreams; of providing quality, affordable healthcare across the length and breadth of the country, providing credit to the underprivileged and democratising the benefits of technology to reduce disparity and environment protection. He is loving the time he can spend with the family and the time he now has to do everything, from playing golf to travelling, to listening to music. As Omar Khayyam said,

> “A book of verses underneath the bough
> A flask of wine, a loaf of bread and thou
> Beside me singing in the wilderness
> And wilderness is paradise now.”

Omar Khayyám
(Edward Fitzgerald’s translation of
The Rubaiyat of Omar Khayyam)

JAICO PUBLISHING HOUSE

Elevate Your Life. Transform Your World.

ESTABLISHED IN 1946, Jaico Publishing House is home to world-transforming authors such as Sri Sri Paramahansa Yogananda, Osho, the Dalai Lama, Sri Sri Ravi Shankar, Sadhguru, Robin Sharma, Deepak Chopra, Jack Canfield, Eknath Easwaran, Devdutt Pattanaik, Khushwant Singh, John Maxwell, Brian Tracy, and Stephen Hawking.

Our late founder Mr. Jaman Shah first established Jaico as a book distribution company. Sensing that independence was around the corner, he aptly named his company Jaico ('Jai' means victory in Hindi). In order to service the significant demand for affordable books in a developing nation, Mr. Shah initiated Jaico's own publications. Jaico was India's first publisher of paperback books in the English language.

While self-help, religion and philosophy, mind/body/spirit, and business titles form the cornerstone of our non-fiction list, we publish an exciting range of travel, current affairs, biography, and popular science books as well. Our renewed focus on popular fiction is evident in our new titles by a host of fresh young talent from India and abroad. Jaico's recently established translations division translates selected English content into nine regional languages.

Jaico distributes its own titles. With its headquarters in Mumbai, Jaico has branches in Ahmedabad, Bangalore, Chennai, Delhi, Hyderabad, and Kolkata.

SINCE 1946

www.ingramcontent.com/pod-product-compliance
Ingram Content Group UK Ltd.
Pitfield, Milton Keynes, MK11 3LW, UK
UKHW021704190726
13853UKWH00001B/415

9 789393 559630